The Canal Duke's Collieries

Since the first edition of this book was published in 1982, new material has been made available and as a result, the text has been extensively revised for this second edition, and more illustrations have been included. 'The Canal Duke's Collieries' is about the hidden side of Worsley's heritage, which is now receiving the wider appreciation it deserves.

This edition is dedicated to the memory of the late Frank Mullineux

Preface

This survey covers the coal mining enterprises of the 3rd Duke of Bridgewater and his succeeding Trust. It outlines the extent, methods and social consequences of the operations carried out at Worsley, near Manchester, during the years 1760-1900.

The book is set out in chronological order, although digressions are necessary to illustrate certain points. It is for the general reader as well as the specialist historian; for those who wish to know more about their locality, or how one of the largest pre-nationalisation coal mining empires grew, rather than for the mining engineer. With these points in mind, geographical locations are given their modern names. Further to assist the reader, the development maps are produced over a standard grid of the most salient modern features.

Little mention is made of the more widely known canals which were constructed during the same period. These are referred to only when the two undertakings coincide in relation to the shipment of coal. For a greater part of their formative years, both the canals and the mines were under the same management, and it must be remembered that the one was originally there to serve the other.

Glen Atkinson, Worsley

Contents

Acknowledgements

During the compiling of this study I was glad of the help of my wife, Nancy, and the constant encouragement of Elsie and the late Frank Mullineux. I am grateful to Frank for advice, loan of material, and for checking the manuscript. Thanks are also due to Mrs Barbara Elwell and Mrs Vivienne Edwards for producing a typescript.

For assistance with research, my thanks are due to the Archivist and staff of the County Record Office, Preston; the Archivist and staff of the County Record Office, Northampton; the National Coal Board Records when at Anderton House, Lowton; the Curator and staff of the Lancashire Mining Museum, Salford; Mr Frank Walsh for loan of material and advice; the late Mr J Lane for his extensive notes on the subject and the benefit of his local mining knowledge.

Many of the photographs are from the Frank Mullineux Collection; others have been kindly provided by the Lancashire Mining Museum, Chetham's Library, Salford Local History Library and Mr F Walsh.

Worsley and Mining before 1760

At the start of the eighteenth century, before the Canal Duke's activities and the centralisation of industry, Worsley was still mainly agricultural. As in most English villages at this time, specialist tradesmen would supply the everyday needs of the people, with very few consumer goods being brought into the area. Cottage industry was a very important addition to the local economy and hand-operated textile machinery predominated.

Coal mining was a secondary industry until the mid-eighteenth century. Accounts of coal-getting are recorded as early as 1376, and by 1500 regular leases for coal-getting were being made in Worsley and Little Hulton. In early times there were many reasons why turf, or peat, and wood fuels were preferred to coal. In Lancashire, with the extensive mosses where most tenants had turbary rights, turf was easily procurable and popular belief was that it grew, thus the supply was thought to be inexhaustible. In buildings without proper chimneys, the more aromatic smoke of turf would have been preferable to the belchings of sulphurous smoke produced by the poor quality coal mined at the time. The cost of transport was also against large scale use of coal in towns. The only regular users on a commercial basis were smiths and limeburners, who required fuel that would burn hotter than turf. Other trades which gradually turned to coal, particularly in the North of England, were brewing and dyeing.

Until well into the eighteenth century, Worsley was an agricultural island surrounded by inhospitable moss and moorland. Glacial deposits of boulder clay over the sandstones formed impervious basins to the south and north east. These gave rise to the great Chat and Kearsley mosses, whilst the non-deposited land to the north gave rough moorland with light soil cover. The Lancashire mosses may better be described as gigantic bogs which, over most of their surface, would only support a man's weight when he was wearing boards strapped to

his feet like snowshoes. The northern Walkden moor was passable to animals, although of little use agriculturally.

Thus the outlying districts of Worsley offered poor prospects for farming, compared to the fertile basin at the centre of the estate. These natural features influenced early lines of communication. A network of roads and tracks served the several communities, skirting the more fearsome obstacles until the reclamation projects of the eighteenth century reduced these problems. In the middle of the wastelands lay Worsley, with its farming and administrative centres at the Halls and their demesne farms. By the

end of the sixteenth century the process of land clearance had progressed to the limits of the mosslands. The scattered nature of the population is evident from maps drawn as late as 1720.

It is most likely that the first British settlement at Worsley was formed during the early Saxon age. Worsley is taken to mean 'a place cleared', and over the following centuries there were many variations in the spelling, of which Workedsleigh is typical. The Romans built two roads across the area. The main route from Manchester to Warrington ran through the northern part of Eccles and through Worsley, passing the present Drywood Hall and leaving the area through Boothstown. Another, less important, Roman road ran further to the north, along

The Worsley area on Yates's map of Lancashire, 1786

the line of the present A6 road at Walkden.

During the feudal period following the Norman conquest, Worsley became a true estate; a manor granted to the Barton family. For the next few centuries a gradual process of sub-division occurred to accommodate dominant family members. The smaller estates of Wharton, Kempnough and Wardley formed in the thirteenth century and Boothstown was the last of these partition gifts, early in the fourteenth century. In addition to the estate, there was the manor of Middle Hulton which, in 1311, was received in an exchange of lands with Richard Hulton.

The first member of the Barton family to receive the estate changed his name to de Worsley to signify ownership and the main estate stayed in the hands of his descendants until the late fourteenth century. Subsequent owners were the Masseys of Tatton and, by the late sixteenth century, the Breretons, and Dorothy Egerton married into this family. On re-marriage she became Dame Dorothy Leigh, and endowed a charity, still distributed in Worsley. The estate remained in her family until 1923.

The surrounding districts were in the hands of several owners, with land holdings following the old manor boundaries fairly closely. Part of Little Hulton was owned by the Kenyon family based at the Old Hall at Peel, whereas the eastern part of the Peel estate was inherited in 1737 by Sir Joseph Yates, who was installed at the new Peel Hall. Hulton Park was the seat of the Hultons, Lords of the Over Hulton estate. Scattered piecemeal throughout the area were lands belonging to the Reverend W Bagot, the largest being in Middle Hulton and in Walkden, in the centre of the Worsley manor. Farnworth from the 13th century was owned by the Levers and the Hultons, though the Levers eventually sold the south western section to the Bridgeman family.

Any enterprise needing to move goods in bulk suffered transport difficulties in the early eighteenth century. Goods could only be carried by pack horse or river. The coal trade from Worsley was served by the long pack horse trains, with each horse limited to about two-and-a-half hundredweight. Local uses were made of the Irwell and Mersey rivers, but often insufficient water defeated navigation.

At the start of the eighteenth century Manchester was already becoming industrialised and was growing rapidly. Its premises developed an insatiable appetite for fuel and eventually a proposal to make navigable the rivers into Manchester was presented to Parliament. In outline, the plan was to control the water flow of the Mersey and the Irwell by flash locks. Work was substantially complete by 1735 and its effects on the economics of transport were enormous; carriage costs from Liverpool to Manchester tumbled from £2 to 62.5 pence per ton, compared with pack horses. Despite the improvements, the waterway had many snags, particularly when times of drought played havoc with haulage schedules.

Necessity also forced improvements upon the roads and a system of turnpike trusts was established. These trusts improved the roads, drawing their finance by charging tolls to the users. As a result of this competition, further concessions to regular users were offered by the navigation proprietors, who still had a virtual monopoly of transport into Manchester.

The Egerton estate suffered from this stranglehold. Coal mining was one of the revenue-earning activities at Worsley and, as the coal had to be transported to its users in Manchester, the navigation did very well out of the venture. Dissatisfaction with the constant bleeding of profits led to investigations into other means of transport. A consortium of Manchester businessmen sought an Act of Parliament to make navigable the Worsley Brook. With Earl Scroop Egerton as a Commissioner, sanction was received in 1737. The scheme was to improve the brook from Boothstown to Barton on the Mersey & Irwell Navigation, and there were further plans to construct a tramway from the Worsley mines to the Boothstown end of the brook. However, work on the scheme was never started.

As the years passed, Manchester grew rapidly and the demand for fuel to feed the growing industries was enormous. A further group of Manchester businessmen proposed a true canal from the Wigan coalfield, through Leigh, Worsley and Salford. A Bill was presented to Parliament in 1754, but opposition was immense from

The Old Hall, Worsley, where canal and mining projects were planned

landowners, with the exception of the Egertons, who welcomed it. Again the scheme fell through, leaving the transport system unchanged, but doubtless giving some ideas to the future young Duke at Worsley.

The owner of land is deemed to own everything under the land with the exception of precious metals and, recently, coal. Thus minerals are property and permission is needed for them to be removed. Tenants on estates were not allowed to extract coal without paying for the privilege, although, until the late eighteenth century, charges were within the reach of the more prosperous tenants, who exploited the outcrops. The deeper seams were left to the landlords, or those with the capital to reach them. At this stage in the development of mining, where capital investment was needed and appreciable sums could be made from allowing others to mine one's coal, full legal protection of capital and mineral assets became necessary. From a simple written agreement between parties grew the comprehensive leases of the coalfields. With the protection of both parties in mind, the clauses generally covered the following points:

The area of land to be leased and the seams included were defined. A fixed annual rent was normally paid, together with a royalty on the amount of coal mined per year. It became usual to lease coal on the basis of a sum per foot thickness of the seam per acre worked. The 'Cheshire acre' (10,240 square yards - a statute acre is 4,840 square yards) was used almost exclusively in the Lancashire coalfield and known as the customary acre. Access was guaranteed for the lessee, both in surface and underground wayleaves, with provision for surface buildings. Further clauses would indicate penalties for default, the duration of the lease and the conditions of its conclusion. It became common to exclude from royalty payment any coal consumed in working the mine. A further development specified conducting the enterprise in a workmanlike manner, leaving adequate support for the surface and barriers between adjacent property. Surveys were allowed by

the lessees to check this had been done, and to assess the amount of coal got.

The craft of mining coal also developed from the domestic quarryings at outcrops to working deeper seams. 'Bell pits' or 'day holes' were the method of extraction in the early 1600s. These were shallow shafts sunk on the dip side of the outcrop, and the coal was worked in feeble daylight - hence the name - until water problems or the threat of collapse and poor ventilation forced their abandonment. A further shaft would then be sunk nearby and the process repeated. With the experience gained in roof support, the period of production of a shaft was extended, and the need to work the coal in a regular manner evolved. The usual Lancashire method was by pillar and stall, which involved cutting a roadway in the coal from the shaft and opening stalls into the seam at regular intervals, leaving walls of coal to support the roof. When maximum coal had been got from the stalls, the pillars could be removed in an orderly retreat to the shaft. This method was in fairly general use by the late 1600s.

There was always a risk when siting a shaft that it would not hit a seam, particularly when the

outcrop was not well defined or covered with an over-deposit. The introduction of test boring with percussive drills and augers in the early 1700s must have given greater confidence in positioning, by giving accurate data to work on.

Miners' tools both for sinking shafts and getting coal were few and simple. A percussion drill and hammer with black powder was used for shaft sinking; picks and spades, originally of wood with iron tips, got the coal by undercutting the seam and parting it from the face with wedges. It must be remembered that coal was only saleable in fairly large lumps until well into the twentieth century. These lumps would be stacked on a sledge and dragged to the shaft to be wound to the surface by windlass. A later development was the horse engine, or gin, used to raise the baskets of coal to the surface, the area round the mouth of the shaft being known as the pit bank. Although common in other areas, it does not seem that the practice of carrying coal on people's backs up a ladder in the shaft was used to any great degree at any Worsley pits.

Ladder access to the workings for personnel was extensively used up to the end of the nineteenth century. These 'ladder pits' had the

Wardley Hall, built on one of the smaller Worsley estates in the early sixteenth century

ladders arranged in flights, with landings or stages at intervals. The experience gained in sinking workings became essential knowledge by the late seventeenth century, as shallow outcrops were exhausted and deeper reserves had to be developed. At this stage, mining became a true craft; skill was necessary to combat the colliers' enemies of water and gas, which were met with in increasing quantities.

From the technical side, these bugbears of drainage and ventilation were to trouble mining engineers for as long as the Worsley coalfield was worked. The solutions of different generations of miners were the same; drain the water and dilute the gas by ventilation. Only the technology used differed, especially after the development of the steam engine.

The gases colliers have to contend with are of two types. One, lighter than air, is fire-damp or methane; the other, heavier than air, was called black-damp (carbon monoxide). Fire-damp was the most prevalent in the shallow Worsley pits. A recognised treatment for someone overcome with gas was to place their head in a hole in the floor, in the hope that the fresher air would revive them. In the 'day hole' pits, ventilation was at its crudest. The usual solution was for colliers to take turns at beating the gas out by flapping a jacket. Eventually it was realised that two shafts joined by a tunnel on an incline would produce a small, natural draught, usually sufficient to clear all but the most serious influxes of gas.

Accumulations of water were more difficult to remove. The regular method was simply to hoist it up the shaft in leather or iron buckets and discharge it into a surface drain. This laborious work was often undertaken during the night, to avoid congestion in the shaft during the working shift. It was also necessary to prevent undue build-up during lengthy stoppages at weekends. Records show the paying of double time for night and weekend water winding from a very early date. When shafts were sunk to greater depths, ground pressure in loose strata caused further influxes of water. The answer was to line the shaft

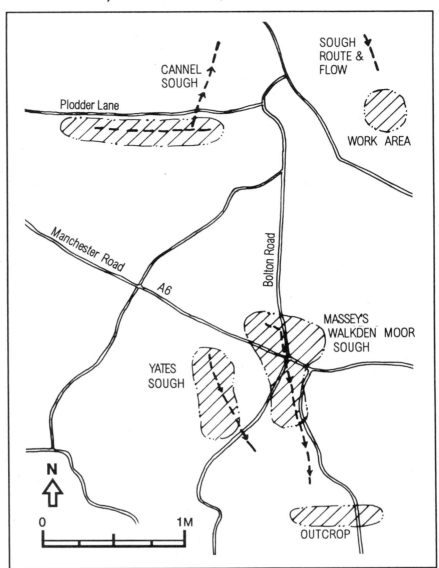

Coal workings before 1760

completely with timber. This gave colliers the impression of being in a barrel, thus giving the name 'tubbing' to shaft lining of any material.

Direct hoisting was an expensive way of removing water in deeper pits. The solution came from the Pennine valleys, in whose steep sides 'water looses' or culverts were constructed. These small tunnels ran from the workings to a point lower down the valley, allowing the water to run away by gravity. In the valleys these were short, but in the flatter districts of central and south Lancashire the culverts had to run a much greater distance before an outlet lower than the workings could be reached. However, by the later seventeenth century the construction of such drainage soughs became economic.

It is certain that the Romans used coal fuel during their stay in Lancashire. Ashes have been found in several of their stations, particularly at Castlefield in Manchester, although where this was mined is unknown. That coal mining took place in the Worsley area is well documented. In a court case of 1376, when Sir Geoffrey de Worsley was arrested for debt, an inventory of possession was made. This included a profit for digging and selling sea coals of 75p a year. Also in the manor records is the tenants' rent, paid at 35p per year, for the 'coal mole', or ground to mine on.

During the sixteenth century, mining continued to supply, intermittently, a small domestic market. Records show that the Hultons frequently contracted leases with tenants in Little Hulton. In 1575, a lease was concluded concerning a place called Feighing Slack, indicative of the method of mining by feighing, or removing the top soil along the outcrop. The lessee had power to come with carts, carriages and workmen to dig and carry away all the coals found within the demised ground within the peele of Hulton.

In the year 1600 a coal pit was being sunk by Ralph Worsley of Worsley. The accounts show the expenses for sinking the shaft and the merry-making at finding the coal. This pit was some eight-and-a-half yards deep, the sides were well timbered and it was provided with a windlass. The intended output was 25 horse loads per day and the total cost of sinking was 85p. Shaft timbering cost 60p and the labour of three men for two-and-a-half days was 25p. The construction of the windlass was charged at 2.5p, with rope a further 17.5p. The expenses account was closed with the cost of ale at 5p.

Under the Brereton ownership of Worsley in the late sixteenth and seventeenth centuries, mining was much more extensive, seeking other seams and generally becoming organised into a regular industry. The extent of this estate-wide working can be gauged from the inventory attached to Dame Dorothy's will of 1639. Fuel at Worsley Hall was valued at £7, whilst coal, cannel and Basse, already mined and stocked at the pit banks at Middle Hulton, was valued at £140. The mining equipment, comprising windlasses, ropes, chains, sledges and timber, totalled £16. This very benevolent will did not forget those who had laboured to produce the wealth. A codicil gives to the workmen in the coalpits at

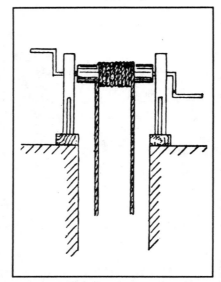 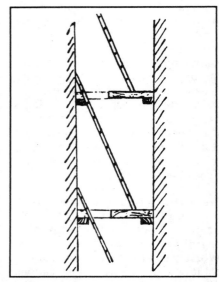

Left: a shaft-top windlass, often used at early pits and pits up to one hundred feet deep. Right: shaft ladders and landings, a common method of access to workings

Middle Hulton 'ten shillings [50p] everyone'.

From these glimpses of mining records in the Worsley coalfields, it is apparent that it was a well developed industry of long standing in the district. It certainly did not appear overnight on the arrival of the Canal Duke. In fact, it saw an influx of enterprise and technology some forty years before he came into his inheritance.

Mining at Worsley developed through the elementary stages already outlined, and probably met demand adequately. However, the upsurge in coal requirements both locally and in nearby Manchester in the 1720s made severe demands on the productive capacity. This growth came during the time of Scroop Egerton, the 4th Earl of Bridgewater, when there were plans to construct a canal to ease the passage of his coal to Manchester. With or without the

proposed canal, improvements were needed if he was to compete in the fuel market at all. With the sanction of the Earl, his Worsley mines agent, John Massey, undertook to improve the output and methods at the pits in his care.

Throughout the preceding centuries the seams had been worked at the outcrop, often in a rather haphazard fashion, leaving the coal in a waterlogged condition. In supplying a mainly domestic market, employment had also been on an impermanent basis. It is likely that the main mining areas were along the outcrop of the Worsley Four Foot seam to the north of the Old Hall, and on the several outcrops in the Parr Fold area of Walkden. The part of the manor unenclosed for agriculture, Walkden Moor, was relatively unexplored.

Massey's problem was to regulate the output at a greater level from accessible seams. In the course of time more continuous work was offered to colliers, although seasonal variations in demand must have caused summer unemployment. To find unflooded coal, other parts of the estate were prospected. The 'gold rush' image conjured up by the word 'prospected' was not far off the mark, as often the only signs of a seam outcrop were in the steep banks of a stream. In the tradition of 'Merrie England', a further ploy was to bribe older inhabitants with ale to remember where the known coal seams lay.

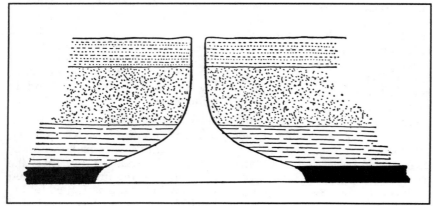

A section of a bell pit, a very early mining method

Finding unflooded coal was a losing battle; the steeply inclined seams and the Lancashire climate conspired against any attempt to keep the pits clear by winding water. Eventually it became an economic necessity to deal with the water problem by capital expense. The decision was taken to construct a drainage sough in Worsley. This was started in 1729, and sited to give a low fall, and hence maximum depth where it was needed, under the coal. Originally planned to be of modest size, to be economic it had to serve the maximum number of pits. The Parr Fold area of Walkden was chosen, as there three seams, the Binn, Croumbouke and Brassey, outcropped within 300 yards of each other. Here the land starts to rise more steeply to the north from a shallow valley north of Ladyhill Ridge overlooking Worsley Village.

Hampered by land contours and the need to avoid trespass on others' land, the plan was to outfall into Kempnough Brook near Greenleach Lane, making use of the shallow valley. A watercourse followed this valley westwards, to a point north of Old Hall Lane where a sharp turn to the north was made. To maintain the advantage of the fall, this section was built in shallow culvert, meandering to avoid trespassing at Edgefold and to bring it closer to Walkden Road. The watercourse continued in gradually deepening culvert to

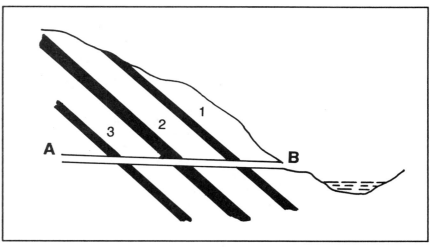

The principle of a sough, or adit level, draining coal seams. The water flows from A to B

Edgefold where, with the rise in surface level, it continued north underground as a tunnel closely following the west side of Walkden Road until the seams were intercepted.

Built in primitive conditions, the tunnel was only large enough for its workers to gain access. It was very roughly made by rock drilling and shoring in softer ground, which gave endless trouble in maintenance. Access shafts were sunk as required. Skilful surveying was its saving grace, giving a fall of some 1 in 400 to a surface outfall at about 160 feet above Ordnance datum. The watercourse allowed pits of about 40 feet depth to be drained at Parr Fold. In its original form, the sough was approximately 1,100

yards long, of which about 600 were fully underground.

The sough served its purpose - it drained away the water which had percolated from the surface, lowered the water table in its vicinity and allowed access to the coal. To mine deeper reserves, water winding was resorted to, with the advantage of winding only to the sough instead of to the surface. This saved the effort of lifting between 20 and 30 feet in the Edgefold area. In all, about ten shafts were connected with the sough in its original form, most of them still having to resort to water winding. There were also maintenance problems with the construction materials - wooden planks when constantly wet are hardly a permanent retainer under earth pressure. Frequent collapses occurred and removing them was a very dangerous job. It often involved a chain of men lying on their stomachs, passing the rubble back hand to hand, in fear of a sudden flood when the pent-up water was released.

Regular inspections were made by a collier wading down through the sludge to examine the state of the sides. This inspector was supplied with a flannel shirt against the wet and cold of the journey - an early form of protective clothing! The sludge was periodically removed and the workers rewarded with ale. Handouts of beer were a regular feature whenever a special effort of any sort was needed; whether this was as an inducement or a reward is not recorded. Some repairs were made in brickwork,

The horse gin, an early mechanical coal winding method which was common at Worsley

although few lengths were so treated.

The shallowness of the sough really defeated its purpose of gravity discharge. In the steeply-inclined seams of Worsley it was preferable to work uphill from the shaft bottom so that the coal could be sledged downhill to the shaft. Water also collected here. Extensions were therefore planned to lengthen the sough further north to cut into the same seams of Binn, Croumbouke and Brassey again, to the north of Shaving Lane fault. Owing to land rise, these would be intercepted at a much deeper level.

This was done, involving about 450 yards of tunnelling to the Binn seam, just south of Walkden town centre. The route runs to the east of Memorial Road, passing under Walkden centre and to the west of Bolton Road, where it was eventually finished at the junction of Ashton Field Drive and Campbell Way. This extension had the advantage of giving a drainage depth of 90 feet at the Binn seam, increasing to about 120 feet at the Seven Feet seam where it terminated. Progress was such that redundant shafts were being filled in Walkden centre by 1732.

For the time it was constructed, this was a fair achievement, with about 1,350 yards of tunnelling and some 500 yards of shallow culvert, all of low fall. Shorter than some soughs made in other coalfields, it served the limited needs of Worsley. Again a great number of shafts made use of it, having little need to wind water with this depth of drainage. Extensive working took place in

the seams intercepted and small branch soughs were made to drain along the lateral axis of seams.

The latter half of the seventeenth century saw parallel developments in adjoining areas belonging to other landowners. With the encouragement of rising demand in Bolton, the coalfield owned by the Bridgemans received its share of attention. The Cannel, Plodder and Dean Moor seams were worked extensively by outcrop means until water problems made recourse to a drain sough essential. This sough was apparently the earliest in the district, as work is believed to have commenced in 1647.

Known as Dixon Green or Cannel sough, its focal point was at Dixon Green. From there the sough ran roughly northwards to outfall into a surface brook at Doe Hey Clough at Moses Gate. This was a distance of 1,100 yards and gave a drainage advantage of about 60 feet at Dixon Green. Many shafts were connected to the sough along its length where water winding had been necessary. Branch arms were driven from Dixon Green along the Cannel seam to drain it. The eastern arm was short, whilst the western one was later lengthened to over one-and-a-half miles. This arm runs almost parallel with Plodder Lane but about 150 yards to the south. The extent of mining in the earlier period is difficult to establish owing to the later extensions, but it was probably fairly well developed to justify building the sough.

By 1737 Sir Joseph Yates became owner of Peel estate in Little Hulton and began to make use of

the mineral wealth beneath it. He also leased other parts of Peel for mining. The terms of the lease were many, but the outline was that the coal was to be mined to a depth from the outcrop that was adequately drained by the sough he was making in Peel. The seams involved were the second series of the Binn, Croumbouke and Brassey, on a royalty payment of 3p per twenty-four standard baskets. The mining rights of Common Head Farm were also leased by Yates in 1737. It would appear that this lease was taken with the idea of having access to the proposed Worsley Brook canal, as the royalty was to increase if the canal was made.

From its outfall into Knocket Wall Brook between Ellenbrook and Mather Fold, the shallow culvert gradually deepened to a tunnel sited to the west of the hamlet of Providence and through the leased seams on the western side of Hilton Lane. The sough terminated on the Seven Feet seam near Engine Fold, where its depth was 37 yards from the surface, a very useful drainage advantage. The deeper section from Mather Fold is about 1,000 yards long, a not inconsiderable undertaking. Extensive working with related access shafts took place along the intercepted seams.

Coal mining then was a well organised industry, technologically not too far out of line with national developments. When considered in relation to the existing markets on the threshold of the steam age, it had probably developed as well as it could. It was only awaiting the transport and industrial revolution, shortly to break, to give greater stimulus to its growth.

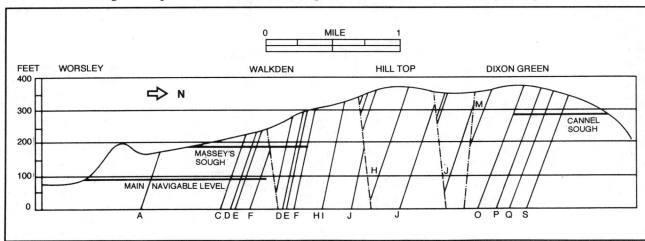

A geological section from Worsley to Dixon Green (the vertical scale has been exaggerated)

Colliery improvements and the Duke's waterways

The Canal Duke was unusual in many respects. He was one of the first members of the landed gentry actually to participate in the mining of his estates at a period when industry was considered not quite the socially accepted occupation of a nobleman. Francis Egerton was a visionary who turned his ideas to one end, the development of his inherited estates, and he applied himself to the task as diligently as he expected his staff to do. For a long period he lived perhaps more frugally than his senior employees in order to re-invest as much capital as possible in the great industrial gamble that finally paid off.

Socially well connected, the Egerton dynasty was founded by Thomas the Baron of Ellesmere, Lord Chancellor, who had ambitions towards an earldom but never achieved the honour. His son John, the purchaser of the Worsley estates, received the title of First Earl of Bridgewater and retained the baronetcy. Two more John Egertons succeeded as earls, the last dying in 1701. Scroop, the fourth earl, father of thirteen, received the accolade of a dukedom in 1720. He died in 1745. Infant mortality plagued the Egertons in the form of consumption and it was John, the fourth son, who received the second dukedom. It was short lived, as John succumbed to the disease in 1748.

The family had never considered Francis, the fifth and youngest son, born in 1736, as likely to attain succession. He was a sickly, almost illiterate child, thought to be mentally defective. Grudgingly declared fit to succeed to the title, he was placed under the guardianship of Samuel Egerton, the Duke of Bedford, and the Earl Gower. These worthies, trying to make the best of the job, packed Francis off to Eton for a few years. From Eton he was sent on the Grand Tour of Europe under the care of a classical scholar.

On returning to England, the young Duke settled in at his London home to a life of supervising his estates with the advice of his agents; horse racing, and several love affairs. Francis was certainly one of the young bloods of the town, and one of the leading lights of the racing community at Newmarket, where he kept his own stable. He also rode himself, wearing his own colours of blue and silver. His first love affair was with a Miss Jane Revell, but the expected wedding

John Gilbert, land agent and mining engineer

never happened as she abandoned Francis for another young heir. The second, equally disastrous, affair was with the widowed Duchess Elizabeth Hamilton. Although they were publicly engaged, the marriage failed to take place. Unsuccessful in love, Francis retired, the better to mature his industrial plans, the foundations of which had been laid whilst these love affairs had been progressing.

Initially, as Francis Egerton was still under a guardianship, and in line with the usual practice of running landed estates, competent staff had to be found. Earl Gower was able to use his influence to secure the appointment of his own agent, Thomas Gilbert, to supervise the young Duke's interests and this began a partnership that was to last a lifetime. The Gilberts were of Staffordshire squire stock, with an estate at Cotton. Of the two brothers, Thomas, the elder, was a lawyer and took up estate management under Earl Gower. John Gilbert had trained as an engineer but on the death of their father returned to supervise their own property. Under the direction of his brother, John had served the Duke on practical estate matters since 1753.

In 1757 Francis Egerton came into his full inheritance unhindered by any guardianship, and shouldered complete responsibility for all his estates. The changes were such that Thomas Gilbert nominally returned

The Navigable Level entrance tunnel, drained for repair and dredged of sludge

to Cotton from Ashridge, whereupon John moved to Worsley as factor to the estate there, under his brother. He moved into the Old Hall with his family in July. From there he studied the land and mines and discussed with the Duke and his brother the possibilities for improvements. They all agreed on the need for efficient transport. The previous attempts in the district to introduce canals, the success of the river improvements, and the fact that Earl Gower had canal plans well advanced made their decision to make a canal from Worsley to Manchester a logical one.

When John Gilbert first came to live in Worsley the surface canal was still completely in the future. The demand for fuel locally and in Manchester was increasing. The intended canal would increase the requirements still further, so the pits had to be ready and able to supply them. John set about a programme of putting the works in good order and introducing methods that were new to Worsley. By this time technology had partially overtaken mining as practised there, and although the methods were adequate for previous generations, they would not do for the intended output. The sough as the focus of existing works came in for attention, its accumulations of silt were cleared and several of its more doubtful sections of arch secured with brickwork. Continuous extension to the north to tap and dry the untouched seams in the Ashton's Field area was planned and put in hand. On the deeper pits, horse gins for winding replaced windlasses to improve performance. Steam pumps were experimented with and may have been introduced to allow better exploitation of the seams both below the sough and at pits along the Four Foot seam near the Old Hall. The improvement of these and new sinkings there saved cartage to the intended canal terminus. To gain precise geological information, boreholes were made with both percussive and auger drills and these gave data on seams below present workings and in virgin ground.

A survey of the land gave information for laying out the intended canal, most importantly

The original (east) Level entrance, pre-1769, and part of the description from Arthur Young's 'Six Months Tour through the North of England' (1770)

The great curiofity at *Worfley* is the tunnel, which is a fubterraneous canal hewn out of the rock to a great length (near a mile,) and extends into the heart of the coal mines. The view, Plate VII. exhibits the mouth of it, and likewife the quarry works around it.
 A. The navigation.
 B. The mouth of the tunnel, with large doors to open and fhut.
 C. The quarry.
 D. A crane of a very curious conftruction, for heaving the ftones out of the quarry into the barges.
 E. Ropes that keep the crane in its perpendicular pofition.
 The water in the tunnel is upon the level of that in the canal, being the fame, fo that the boats loaded with coals come out of the very mine itfelf.

confirming that it would be possible to approach Manchester without using many locks. A terminus at Worsley village would avoid the rise of land to the north towards Walkden, where most of the pits were. In deciding upon the most economic method of getting the coal to the canal, the choice was between pack horses, carts and railed wagon ways. Gilbert had his borehole surveys available as well as the normal topographical ones and a study of these gave the idea which solved most of the problems at one go.

The answer was to continue the canal underground at the same level. This solution would provide an economic method of transport for the coal, and it would continue the work of the sough at a deeper level, with the water being used to feed the canal.

With these outline plans made, the route of the canal became finalised. The intention was to reach towards Liverpool as well as Manchester and a construction Bill was presented to Parliament. This proposed that a canal be allowed from Hollins Green on the Mersey near Irlam, via Worsley, through to Salford on the River Irwell. At this stage the Duke, realising the immense capital outlay needed to finance these undertakings, made

a very personal contribution. He reduced his private expenditure to £400 per year and, wishing to keep fully in touch with the event he had started, adopted a lifestyle of travelling between his estates and London in the company of Thomas Gilbert. As a gambler, perhaps he saw this reduction in lifestyle as his stake money. Before finally leaving society and before severe financial restrictions set in, Francis held a large ball in London to celebrate the likely passing of the Canal Bill.

The Act was obtained in March 1759 and work started on the canal immediately. It was rapidly cut west to Boothstown and east to Patricroft. Here the intention was to contour along the north bank of the Irwell to Salford.

About this time another remarkable person came to

Worsley, partly by the influence of Earl Gower. James Brindley was engaged as a consulting engineer on the canal project. Soon a change was made in the route; the canal was to cross the Irwell by aqueduct and approach Manchester from the south. Presented to Parliament in January 1760, the change was sanctioned in March that year and the Barton Aqueduct was substantially complete in July 1761. As an interim measure, an outlet for Worsley coal involved craning it over the side of the aqueduct to boats on the Mersey & Irwell Navigation below, and thence to Manchester. When the canal reached Cornbrook in 1763, temporary coal distribution took place there until the terminal at Castlefield was completed in 1764.

Whilst this work was going on, the route of the proposed canal to Runcorn on the Mersey was under survey. Intense opposition arose from landowners, but the plan received sanction in March 1762. Protracted land deals and engineering problems delayed the work so that this stretch of canal took over ten years in the making.

Between the years 1759 and 1762 Worsley underwent its own industrial revolution, an upheaval in pace of life, methods and scale of doing things. All the ingredients of wholesale change were there, many new trades were introduced and there was vast expansion of the old. This was fully reflected in the scene at Worsley village, the centre of operations, where the physical effects of several schemes were seen virtually all at once. The new canal had to be dug, the pits improved and worked more extensively, and the new navigable sough started. All this industry

Francis Egerton, His Grace the Third Duke of Bridgewater - The Canal Duke

needed back-up services in the form of workshops for the civil and mechanical engineers as well as the newly required boat-building services. In the course of these few years Worsley became almost a vast construction site where John Gilbert established the order of events and their location, trying to keep everything in schedule with his master plan. To allow such a simultaneous increase of effort on many projects, larger numbers of workers were needed, but as the initial tide of canal making moved away from Worsley the majority of labourers moved with it.

Once the idea of the canal continuing underground as the main improvement to the mines was conceived, no time was lost in making a start on it. Work was in hand whilst the final plans were being made for the surface canal. To avoid confusion, the underground canal is better referred to by the colliery staff's name for it, 'The Level' or 'the Navigable Level'. In outline, the plan was to tunnel into the sandstone ridge which rose steeply from the Cheshire plain. From the canal level at 82 feet above sea level, a tunnel started in the village near the corn mill and headed northwards into the rock. Eight feet wide, its roughly elliptical arch gave four feet of headroom, with also four feet of water. This continued until the first workable coal seam was intercepted 770

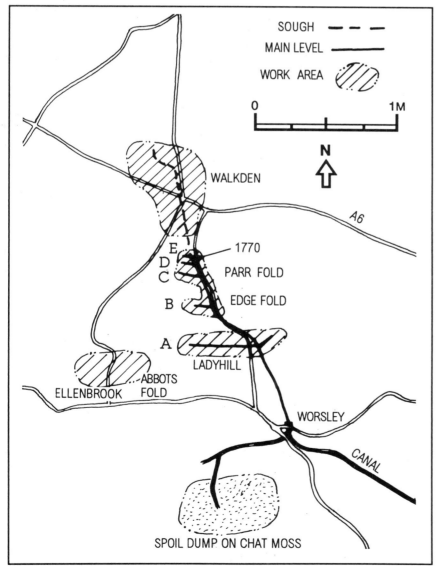

Mining development 1760-1770 (See seam sequence chart, page 2)

yards from the outfall. Its depth gave a drainage depth advantage of 35 yards over the old sough. As the Four Feet seam had never been served by the sough, the level served a greater workable area.

Work got under way on the level and difficulties soon arose. In April 1759, a band of hard rock was reached and the disheartened miners struck. Only a promise of continuous payment whatever the rate of progress brought a return to work. Boats to remove spoil were being built later that year and the Level was mentioned in the second Canal Act of 1760 as being under construction. Upon the opening of the Barton Aqueduct in July 1761 a newspaper report states that it was hoped to complete the canal to Manchester before Lady Day (25th March) 'and that in the mean Time the subterraneous Navigation to the Colliery will be perfected'. The amount of manual labour needed in the cramped confines of the tunnel can hardly be imagined. To advance one yard would give fifteen tons of rubble, filling two of the boats used in the work. The

driving was done at piecework rates by small teams of skilled miners. Costs of driving the Level in wages varied according to the strata being worked, but averaged £1-£2 per yard. This sum paid everybody, the labourers as well as the miners. When passing through softer shales, a brick lining was provided at extra cost. Rates of progress obviously varied but the first workable seam, the Four Feet, was reached in 1761.

Although heading almost due north for the first half mile, the Level changes course several times and nowhere is it a dead straight tunnel for long. This winding was necessary to keep the course of the Level on the Duke's own land, or where long leases were held. Minor kinks avoided small geological problems. Extended from the Worsley Four Feet seam, the Level crept north-westwards towards Walkden, where the belt of workable coal lay in the Edgefold area. At each seam intercepted, tunnels were driven into the seam at right angles to the main Level. These branch levels then extended as the coal was

extracted, the general scheme of working being to cut the coal, then move it in sledged baskets to the boats waiting in the branch levels.

With so many developments taking place at the same time, logistic problems could be solved in such a way that the undertakings helped each other. This was especially so with the main Level. Its starting place was a great quarry, where stone for the canal bridges was obtained, and the spoil from the Level was used for smaller masonry and rubble embankments on the canal. The expected flow of mine drainage water to feed the canal was forthcoming, although the extent of the supply was in dispute during the Parliamentary stages of the Cheshire section of the canal. To settle the dispute, the engineer John Smeaton was brought in as arbitrator. His flow measurements proved conclusively that the supply was equal to the task and there was a reserve capacity, as the flow would increase as new seams were tapped. Worsley became the focus of attention for other industrialists and a tourist attraction for the

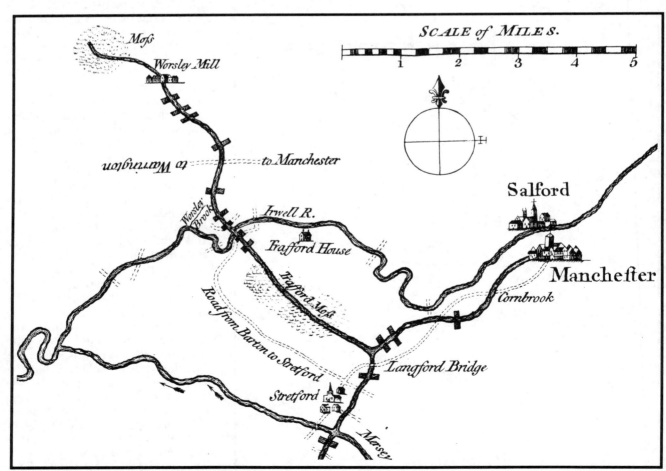

Part of Arthur Young's plan of the Duke of Bridgewater's Canal, published in 1770

learned and the curious. The notes made by these visitors help to give life to the economic accounts surviving in the estate records.

Several of these curious travellers, particularly Sir Joseph Banks and Arthur Young, provide us with a picture of the radically changed Worsley village. From a rustic backwater it had turned into a bustling port and industrial estate. In between the great Level entrance and the canal had sprung up an array of workshops to accommodate all the craftsmen. This central depot served all the Duke's enterprises; here the requirements for materials and equipment were met. Raw materials brought by canal were transformed into building supplies, boats were built and rigged and all the colliery equipment was made at Worsley. Mortar mills, forges and sawyers' yards spread. Vast quantities of bricks and the mortar to lay them were needed in the new works. Lime pits at Bedford in Leigh, and south of the canal near Middlewood, supplied the basis of lime mortar, which was burned and ground near the yard. Even the nails used in boat-building were made there. Most of the processes were undertaken by hand - timber was obtained from the log by hand sawyers - but some powered machinery existed.

The source of power was Worsley Brook. A supply from the dam behind Mill Brow fed a twenty-four-foot diameter water wheel. This certainly earned its keep, as it drove two pairs of corn grinding stones and a boulting mill to separate the flour from the bran. A dual-purpose mortar mill was also driven by the brook. The first section ground the burnt stone to powder, then a further mill with vertical rollers running in a trough mixed the powder with sand and water into mortar. The sand itself was graded by yet another mill driven by the wheel. Here a horizontal, tapered drum with various-size meshes separated the sand and gravels. Also centred upon the yard was the reclamation of Chat Moss, undertaken by boating spoil from the Level to the moss. Gangs of labourers spread it over the peat south of the canal. This labour on the windswept moss earned the place the ironic

nickname of Botany Bay, after the convict settlement in Australia.

The industrial complex at Worsley had grown in the period 1760-65, and the labour force grew with it, yet John Gilbert still had a hand in most of its aspects. The Duke could also be relied upon to keep his eye on the work and his personal supervision gave rise to what is probably the most famous story of him. Regularly noticing the men's tardiness in starting work after the lunch break, he asked the foreman the reason. The one note from the clock at one o'clock was difficult to notice, he was told. The yard clock was soon altered to strike thirteen at one o'clock, a tradition maintained in Worsley public clocks to this day.

During these few years of upheaval and reorganisation, how had the estate itself grown to become industrially viable? With a great rate of output to keep up with the demand for coal, the reserves between the outcrop would soon be exhausted: the system of mining was rapid exploitation at a relatively shallow depth to ensure continuity of supplies. Backed by the canal's success, leases were undertaken for many reasons.

Initially these leases were to safeguard the route of the Navigable Level. In 1759 Mr Starkie of Kempnough contracted

to allow its passage under his land and to allow mining in any seams found. Confidence in the permanency of the work caused the sough, as it was then known, to be allowable 'for ever'. Realising the ease of access to the Four Feet seam, Mr Cooke of Ellenbrook leased his land for coal getting, with soughs to be made as needed. In the midst of the Canal Act proceedings, when expenses had really been cut, sufficient capital was found to re-purchase the Wardley estate to the east of Worsley. This appears to have been left undisturbed until the later years, when it was extensively worked.

The next series of leases involved land to the north of the estate in Farnworth. Here the Cannel and Plodder seams had been worked by their owners past and present. Sir Orlando Bridgeman leased his land containing these seams in 1762, on the understanding that a new, deeper sough would drain them. Again permanency came into the terms; the works were to be made so as to last for five hundred years, although the lease was for only ninety-nine years. Adjacent lands in Farnworth along the lines of these seams were bought or leased in 1764 from smaller landowners.

To consolidate the estate still further, small landowners in Worsley were persuaded to lease

Kempnough Hall, home of the Starkie family in the Duke's lifetime

or sell to the Duke, and several did so in the sixties. At an undetermined date an agreement was reached with Mr Yates of Peel. Although no levels went under his land, mining by the Bridgewater succession certainly went on in the Hilton Lane area for a long time. Several other small leases and purchases in the Ellenbrook area marked the 1770s as a prelude to further expansion in the west.

Ease of transportation of the Four Feet seam coal resulted in a great development in the Boothstown and Tyldesley districts in the 1780s. The Warrington School land off Chaddock Lane and Mr Clowes' land at Booths Hall were leased in 1782 and 1789 respectively. Relatively untouched until then, this field gave great impetus to the workings, particularly the deeper levels. A small but significant lease, that of Sanderson's near Roe Green, also on the Four Feet seam, was contracted in 1785.

The respective terms of these leases give an indication of how landowners gradually realised the true worth of their minerals. The early leases paid peppercorn rents, a return of only one eighth of the value of the coal got and were for ninety-nine years, preventing more advantageous terms being got. At the close of the century rents had grown to substantial sums, returns had grown to one fifth of value or a set amount of money, and terms were shortened to ten or twenty years.

Having connected the Level with the Four Feet seam, it was realised that further extensions to the north would take an appreciable length of time, as nearly three-quarters of a mile of tunnelling would be involved. As a short term measure, along the lines of the general improvements before starting the Level, many pits were worked independently of it. These pits were sunk along the known seams at such distances from the outcrop that the branch level would in due course, the engineers hoped, intercept them. This was particularly so of the Four Feet seam; the closeness to the canal was very much in favour of this development. The pits at Abbots Fold, Ellenbrook, for example, were sunk in the early 1760s about three-quarters of a mile from the

main Level. The solution to the transport problem had a precedent in the 1737 canal scheme. A tramway was laid between the pits and the partially-cut canal to the west of Worsley, near Middlewood. Completed in 1764, this horse-powered railway trundled wagon loads of coal and helped increase outputs.

The early years of the 1760s can be seen as a time of preparation. They are best described in the estate records which refer to 'sinking pits and opening soughs' to make ready for greater expansion. Most parts of the estate were so explored and many pits in the Walkden Moor district were sunk to the requisite depth to await the arrival of the Level. This process of attrition of shallow reserves, with the bulk of the output from the Four Feet seam, continued until the later 1760s.

Within the newly leased district of Deane, preliminary working of the Cannel seam began both at Dixon Green and Watergate. Existing workings were made use of and the old Cannel sough was put to use again after repairs and cleaning out of silt. The intention from the outset was to continue the Navigable Level as far north as Dixon Green, but it was realised in promising the deeper sough that their levels would not coincide.

However, as an interim measure, work proceeded from the terminal point of the old sough. The method was to continue a tunnel along the seam at sough level and then work the coal up the dip of the seam. This tunnel would then serve as a water end drain and assist ventilation. Boats were not used in it; coal was removed via shafts to the surface, from where carts and wagons conveyed it to the respective markets. Although not all of it is attributable to the Duke's collieries, this water end reached a length of nearly one-and-a-quarter miles, with at least ten access shafts.

The first main branch of the Level struck out to the west along the Four Feet seam. It ran under the Ladyhill ridge, virtually following the line of Old Hall Lane. This branch alone eventually reached a length of one-and-three-quarter miles. Several access shafts which provided ventilation intruded into a still agricultural scene. Great and Little Ladyhill pits sent their coal along the Level, and also made their own sales at the pit bank, a system used at most of the Duke's collieries. Geological problems in the line of the Daubhole fault prevented extension of a branch level very far to the east. However, it was soon realised that a tunnel could be cut through the fault north-eastwards, where the seam

An inspection party on the Navigable Level in 1929

could then be worked. This tunnel through rock, not coal, was only used as a means of transport from the workings, which were in the Beesley Green area.

To maintain output in the short term, sources near to Worsley were needed. It was realised that coal getting could take place at a greater depth than the Level, so shafts were sunk or deepened and tunnels along the seam provided a base for the work. As these workings were below the level of gravity discharge, removing water immediately become a headache. These deeper sections were under pumping as early as 1765, a fact recorded by Sir Joseph Banks on his visit to the area.

Steam pumps of the atmospheric and beam types were introduced at Worsley and it is said that James Brindley had a hand in the construction of some of them. He tried to use a wooden stave cylinder in an attempt to reduce premature condensation. Lagging conventional iron cylinders with wood also gave the impression of a barrel, leading to the naming of

Maintenance workers on the Navigable Level at Brassey Junction, near Edgefold, in the 1930s

several collieries 'Tub engine pit'. In the case of Worsley, which had a source of free drainage in the Navigable Level, pumped water would be discharged into the Level to save the additional lift to the surface.

The Navigable Level, now established as lynch pin of the collieries, continued its northwards progress. By about 1767 the small Threequarters seam near Edgefold had been reached and development started. Further driving efforts reached the first series of the repeated seams, the interceptions occurring in March 1770 for the Binn, early 1771 for the Croumbouke and September 1771, when the Brassey was reached. Close proximity to the land boundary prevented any eastwards working, but the western flank eventually had workings reaching over a quarter of a mile into each of these seams.

One of the pits with the longest continuous usage, at Edgefold, was connected to the Level by deepening in 1770. Utilising the drainage provided by the old sough, several new pits, and some others given a new lease of life, worked the second series of Seven Feet and Black seams in Walkden centre, where shafts were sunk adjacent to Manchester Road.

This latter period, 1760-1770, can be seen as one of development and achievement, the result of great foresight and courage. By this time most of the Duke's enterprises were already successful. On the colliery side, although the enterprise was well founded, they were really on the threshold of great achievements.

Maintenance at Brassey Junction a generation after the top photograph was taken

The Navigable Levels and the Inclined Plane

During the early 1770s the Navigable Level had intersected the seams as previously described, and was nearing Walkden and the rich belt of seams there. Although admirable in concept and invaluable in use, the Level suffered from one serious drawback - there was a limit on the number of boats it could take. Coal output had been multiplied many times by the end of the 1760s, but still more was needed. As the workings in the developed seams moved further away from the main tunnel, haulage times increased and traffic jams were frequent.

The jams became a particular problem at the tunnel mouth at Worsley. To ease the situation, work was started on a second entrance tunnel in 1771. Sited about 30 yards west of the existing mouth, this tunnel was driven to converge with the Level some 500 yards from the outlet. For some reason, perhaps to save labour, the new tunnel was made smaller, only six feet six inches wide. Once it was completed, a one-way system was introduced; loaded boats used the new west tunnel and returned empty up the larger east level.

Having further intercepted the first Seven Feet seam in May 1772, Shaving Lane fault was crossed late in 1773 at a distance of one and a half miles from the outfall at Worsley. The Navigable Level had so far progressed at a fairly constant rate, but it was soon to suffer a reduction in its rate of advance. There was a change in policy in the 1770s, relegating the driving of the great Level to a secondary operation. The reasons for the change are lost in the mists of time. Perhaps there was an urgent need to improve the transport of the valuable cannel coal to Worsley. Or it may have been that a substantial rise of land was met as the Level approached Walkden Moor, together with a reduction in the gradient of the seams. In practical terms, this meant that coal had to be carried by sledge for long distances to the branch levels in order to mine it right to the outcrop.

Correspondingly greater efforts in shaft sinking would also be needed.

The outcome was a scheme to enlarge and extend the old Massey sough. In 1773 expenses records show 'widening the old sough across Walkden Moor, to the north, which is proposed to continue to Dixon Green'. This work, which took seven years to complete, gave an Upper Navigable Level thirty-five yards above the main waterway, and aimed primarily at the shallow northern seams. In its completed form it ran for one-and-three-quarter miles from Walkden to Plodder Lane. From this time the original part of the sough between Edgefold and Walkden was abandoned, and drainage water from the new Upper Level flowed down shafts to the Main Level.

In line with the policy of tapping the shallow reserves first, this Upper Level had its heading way in advance of the Main Level. Provisions were being made to load coal into the boats at the Cannel seam intersection in 1780 and the most northerly seam, Dean Moor, had been reached by 1783. During the course of driving the new Upper Level, several workable seams were intercepted. Branch levels started in the Seven Feet near the Barracks and the White seam at Ashton's Field. Further north, the Doe and Five Quarters at Buckley Lane had branches, as did the Plodder seam at Dixon Green.

Problems of getting boats into the higher Level had been foreseen at the outset. It was noted that 'Branches be driven from it, and slanting one which terminates at the surface on the south side of Walkden Moor whereby to put boats down'. This 'day eye' and adjacent shafts were situated in the angle between Ashton Field Street and High Street in Walkden town centre. Made at a dip of one-in-four, it ran south with the dip of the seams to the Upper Level. With the provision of rails and a cradle for hauling boats to and from the surface, new and repaired boats went down and damaged ones came up. After a horizontal landing of forty yards, this incline was later continued downwards to reach the Main Level at a depth of 75 yards.

Materials brought from Worsley yard for the construction of the Upper Level could also be taken down this 'day eye'. However, coal intended for sale at Worsley had to be handled down a shaft to another boat in the Main Level and thence to the canal. The shaft at Barlow Fold was particularly used for this

Waters Meeting, where the two entry tunnels merge, 500 yards inby from the delph to the south

purpose. To meet the need for boats and building materials in the Walkden Moor section, a subsidiary yard grew up around the 'day eye' and a boat yard and reservoir, still known as 'Boat Shed', spread at Campbell Way. A lime burning plant, landsale weighing machine and coke ovens were built on the land between the reservoir and High Street. In the roadway at the junction of High Street and Bolton Road, a workshop known as Rogers shop supplied and repaired the baskets and chains used underground to move the coal. This group of service buildings had been largely completed by 1778.

Whilst the development of the Upper Level took place, working continued on the seams of the second series, with output lowered to the Main Level. This main waterway had developed spasmodically throughout the later 1770s. Leaving Shaving Lane fault, the second series of Binn, Croumbouke and Seven Feet were reached, the Binn seam being worked for 300 yards east and west. The land boundaries allowed the Croumbouke and Seven Feet to be worked some eight hundred yards east, though no west working took place. By 1779 the first Black seam had been reached - 3,425 yards from Worsley. This seam, under the Boatshed at Walkden, had extensive workings on both flanks.

Probably owing to exhaustion after the headlong dash with the Upper Level, the early 1780s saw a period of consolidation. Existing branch levels were developed and extended, a continuous process anyhow. For the first time, to avoid overloading the traffic on the Main Level, a fair proportion of the spoil from driving operations was surface banked near the point of production. Only moderate advances were made on the Main Level; a total of about half a mile to the second Black seam near Ashton's Field.

With the later leases on the Plodder seam in Farnworth, the Upper Level progressed well in that seam and also in the Cannel seam. The longest branch developed in time on the Dean Moor seam. However, the relatively shallow depth and the

effective drainage tended to cause water shortages in the extended upper level branches. The use of water-balance engines at the surface, and particularly in shafts between levels, helped to make the deficiency worse. By 1787 storage reservoirs were needed. Three were built: Boatshed in 1787, Linnyshaw Dam in 1789 and the ten-acre Blackleach in 1794. All were described as being for 'Water to work Bucket engines upon Walkden Moor'.

The 1780s also saw additions to the range of levels deeper than the main artery. Of these, Edgefold pit had the greatest number. In 1787 the shafts were deepened to the Croumbouke seam and branches started. Eventually a short axial level running north connected the shafts with the Brassey and Seven Feet seams. This had a length of 360 yards at a depth of 56 yards below the Main Level. Subsequently a deeper level 83 yards below the Main was added, with an axial length of 290 yards to intercept the same seams. Further south on the Four Feet seam, a lower level sunk by 1790 at Ingles

pit near Ryecroft reached 57 yards deeper than the Main. In later years this became the longest of the deep levels.

In the last full decade of the Duke's influence, development still went on unabated in most sections of the colliery. Existing branch levels were extended where they could be worked economically but some new ventures also started. Wood Pits - the shafts nearest the delph at Worsley - were deepened to reach the Four Feet seam at 75 yards below the Main Level. To increase extraction from this seam further, a wagon road with pony haulage and ventilation shaft ran under Lumber Lane to the workings at Roe Green. Boats and loading stages on the Level received this coal. On the western flank of the coalfield, some independent pits started on the newly leased land in Boothstown.

The Walkden Moor section worked at the Main Level with branches out on to Linnyshaw Moss at Hill Top on the Doe and Windmill seams. North of Ashton's Field, branches and shafts developed on

Brickwork on the Upper Navigable Level. The silting up by ochre deposits is to the original water level and the men are standing on the floor of the tunnel

the second Doe seam. The westerly arm eventually made connection with the cannel workings near Highfield Road. At the close of the century the great artery of the collieries, the Main Level, had struggled its way to Buckley Lane, 5,150 yards from the outlet. Some 17 active shafts connected the Level to the surface, although several more are known to have reached only the Upper Level or to have been used mainly for purposes of construction.

A large proportion of the Deane Moor district did not as yet have Navigable Level connections; the most northerly never did. Such pits relied exclusively on surface wagon transport and to service this outpost of the empire, a small works yard developed at Daubhill, with a stores and smithy to meet day-to-day needs. Dixon Green had a further base depot for services, with another section devoted to coke production. Using the cannel coal, several ovens there met the demand from about 1770. Yet the majority of the branch levels mentioned above had only reached part of their final length.

Throughout the Duke's lifetime coal landsales were made at several places and weighing machines were installed to facilitate the operation. The tramway terminus at Boothstown, the yard at Walkden Moor and Dixon Green were so equipped, but the main coal sales points were obviously along the canal from Worsley to Manchester.

Most of the coal traffic, and also rock waste from tunnel driving, came south down the Level, but there was two-way cargo loaded on it. Vast quantities of building materials and equipment had to go up, and needs for specific grades of fuel meant that Worsley coal was sometimes shipped towards Dixon Green. A bottleneck developed where loads were wound by horse gin or water balance from one level to another. Boats in the Upper Level also had to be manhandled through the 'day eye'.

To overcome these difficulties John Gilbert conceived or copied the idea of connecting the two levels by a self-acting incline, so that complete, loaded boats could be

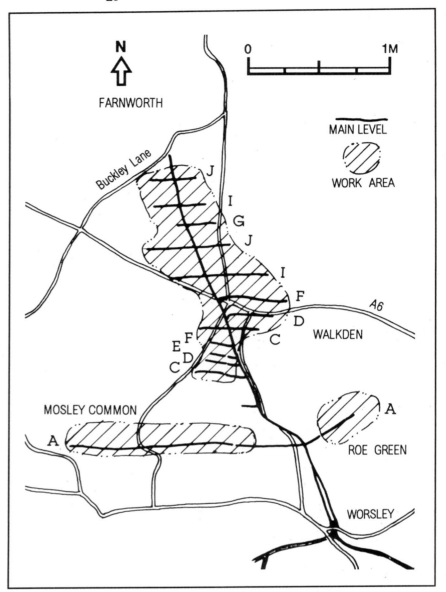

The Main Navigable Level 1770-1800 (See seam sequence chart, page 2)

moved bodily from one to the other. Constructed in the years 1795-97 at Ashton's Field on Walkden Moor, the incline followed the one-in-four dip of a suitable rock stratum, the connection tunnel being some 150 yards in length. Although familiar in many applications, an inclined plane, as it was known, was certainly a novelty when applied to canal boats, particularly underground. Its principle was that a heavily loaded boat at the top of the incline, connected by a rope to a lighter one at the bottom, could be used to haul the lighter one up. The speed of the operation was controlled by a brake on the rope pulley.

Commencing with an 18 yards long lock at the Upper Level, the tunnel continued downbrow for 94

yards. On this stretch it was six yards wide as a double-tracked way for passing boats, then the tunnel continued three yards wide to the Main Level. Headroom in the inclined section was generally 3 yards, increasing to 7 yards at the top locks to accommodate the brake wheel. A rock baulk separated the twin locks, the lower end being in the form of a lay-by in the Main Level. Paddle sluices controlled the flow of water entry and exit in the locks, whilst the lock gates were of the guillotine type, windlass operated. For the length of the locks and the inclined section, cast iron plate rails with small flanges guided the boat cradles. At the junction of single and double way, a movable timber baulk directed the ascending cradle into the correct side; a primitive but effective points mechanism.

Signalling bells, operated by pulling wires, were installed to control operations.

Boats of varying capacities up to twelve tons net were handled by resting them on massive wood and wrought iron cradles fitted with cast iron rollers which mated with the plate rails. The cradles alone weighed some three tons and empty boats were a similar weight. Connecting these cradles needed a two-and-a-half inch diameter rope, cord-wrapped to prevent abrasion, although guide rollers were fitted to the track floor and fairleads at lock corners. Straddling the top locks was the controlling brake drum and rope spindle. Mounted on a horizontal axis, the central brake drum had five-foot diameter cable drums at each side with contra-wound ropes.

This vast contrivance proved to be far from self-acting, at least in initial movement. To overcome this resistance, a spur gear of 372 teeth ran round the rim of the brake drum, with a disengageable pinion of 11 teeth provided on the

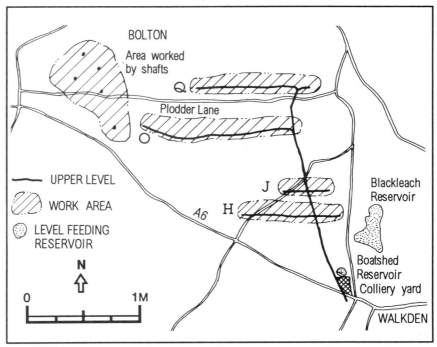

The Upper Navigable Level 1773-1800 (See seam sequence chart, page 2)

spindle of a double-crank windlass. Muscle power certainly featured in the operation, particularly in the unbalanced state when materials were being brought up from the main level.

Considering the physical effort needed by the attendants, the inclined plane is unlikely to have been in continuous operation throughout the day. Its operating cycle is recorded as being about 15 minutes long. In raising materials, however, my estimate is that winding up the full distance, with the low ratio gearing, would take at least half an hour. The inclined plane also meant increased water losses in lockage, so that the supply reservoirs became even more essential. Nevertheless, it proved to be a very successful connection between the levels, being used virtually throughout the active life of the Upper Level.

Unfortunately John Gilbert did not live to see the completion of his inclined plane. He died in 1795, when work had just begun. A gifted engineer and astute businessman, Gilbert had fully vindicated the trust placed in him by the Duke. His efforts and planning, together with a resourceful imagination, had brought off the great gamble. He and the Duke were business partners as well as master and servant: joint enterprises Gilbert became concerned with included other coalfields, transport concerns, and plumbago mining in Cumbria. (This last venture, incidentally, introduced pencil manufacture to Worsley.) No mere financial director, Gilbert oversaw things in a practical way, underground as

The Inclined Plane chamber looking south, showing the junction of the twin tunnels at the top of the incline. The tunnels merge down the incline. The one on the right has been used as a silt dump

well, despite being badly burned in a fire-damp explosion at a Staffordshire pit. There obviously had to be delegation in a concern as diverse as the Duke's, but substantially the decisions were Gilbert's. As a mark of appreciation, his body was buried in the Egerton family vault at Eccles parish church.

With the figurehead gone, a replacement had to be found and business continued. Benjamin Sothern succeeded to the agent's post, with a legacy of outstanding capital projects. That same year Parliament passed the fifth Bridgewater Canal Act, allowing the extension of the canal westward to Leigh. Sothern was the engineer for this, having no doubt done a lot of the preliminary work whilst still John Gilbert's assistant.

As previously noted, it was largely the Duke's own capital that had been used in building the industrial empire. Initially this resulted in a time of great stringency, when both the Duke

and Gilbert toured the country to secure loans for capital. Even the senior employees were 'touched' for a few pounds. His Grace steadfastly refused to mortgage the estate, denying anyone a chance to interfere with his plans. Later, with the canal to Manchester a success, and with further drains on capital in collieries and canals, he did undertake a loan of £25,000 on the security of the canal alone. Financial details are rather tangled, with all the inter-related enterprises. For instance, the Navigable Levels were charged to the canal account, whilst shafts and surface works were separately charged, the two accounts only being united in the mid-1780s. With the exception of a few large loans such as the above, which were rapidly repaid, the whole undertaking was self-financing, a measure of the Duke's and Gilbert's business acumen.

From a colliery point of view, the Duke ran the concern along the lines of a modern supermarket; small returns per unit but a large turnover. The Act authorising the

canal severely limited his financial freedom. It allowed coal to be sold in Manchester at a maximum of two-and-a-half pence per hundredweight, with a maximum carriage charge of twelve-and-a-half pence per ton; these terms to be in force for forty years. Bank sales at the pit appear to have been of the order of one-and-a-half pence per hundredweight for coal, the higher valued cannel fetching two-and-a-half pence, whilst slack sold at one penny. Once the Duke had cornered the market for coal in Manchester, supplies from other coalfields brought in on new canals effectively only kept pace with demand, rather than diminishing the need for Worsley coal. Other markets locally and within reach of land cartage opened up, particularly to Bolton. The Cheshire canal gave access to the salt-working industries and the Mersey Estuary through Runcorn.

The Duke of Bridgewater developed into the first-rate 'character'. The Ducal estates hardly bothered him and he rarely attended the House of Lords except to influence canal business. He was more at home at pit bank or canal wharf, where his homespun, snuff-covered clothes made him blend in easily with the workers. Canal histories give examples of his bluff exchanges with colliers and bystanders and his status as a local patriarch remained largely undiminished in Worsley throughout the following century.

Realising his bachelor state and increasing age, the Duke made preparations for the administration of the estates after his death. He may have been absent from Worsley for most of the year during the last quarter of the century, but there lay his greatest interest. All his preparations for the future centred around preventing anyone interfering with the industrial empire.

In 1800 the Duke drew up his will, the terms of which were to shape the industrial life of Worsley for the next hundred years. Francis Egerton, Duke of Bridgewater, Marquis of Brackley, Baron Ellesmere, died on the 8th March 1803 at Bridgewater House, London, and he was buried in the family vault at Ashridge in Herefordshire.

The Inclined Plane chamber looking north, showing the brake spindle pillar

To be a Collier

Up to the middle of the eighteenth century, conditions at Worsley probably reflected the general state of affairs in agricultural districts throughout the country, with a sharp division between wealth and poverty. At the top of the scale, the senior estate staff lived at the Old Hall. The Egertons themselves rarely visited the area, their main home being at Ashridge. Lower down the social scale the picture was vastly different.

People's standard of living depends most often on the work they do. A village where the employment prospects were farm labouring or coal mining, both at their most primitive, was not likely to provide good conditions of home life. A feature of the employment scene continued in the rather more mixed economy later was the use of the entire family. Wives and children alike joined in the work, in the battle against starvation. All too often, the lot of the wives was daily toil at farm or pit, perpetual pregnancy and domestic needs to be fitted in at the end of the day.

After the departure of the horde of migratory workers who dug the canal, Worsley was still left with a great increase in population. These newcomers were skilled artisans who had responded to a vigorous recruiting campaign by John Gilbert, who travelled to most of the established mining districts in search of colliers and masons. Advertisements were placed in newspapers for 'Sober and dilligent colliers, to whom all reasonable encouragement will be given to work at Worsley'. He was particularly successful in recruiting in Derby, Staffordshire, Shropshire and Cumberland. To attract workers of any ability, housing had to be available, so cottages were built for the colliers and other estate workers.

These cottages were erected to a fairly standard design in the various parts of the estate as needed. Although fairly cheaply built - thirty were made for £1,545 in 1790 - many still stand, often much modified from their original form of isolated, brick, two-up-two-down terraces. Although the population had increased dramatically, the inhabitants still numbered under 5,000 in 1790, by which time the estate contained about 800 houses. The main groupings were in Worsley village, round the yard, and there were several clusters near Walkden and at Dixon Green.

Each little community gained its own identity, characterised by a nickname. A lot of Staffordshire workers lived in Tup Row; other new arrivals soon named their row The Barracks. Half Crown Row owed its name to suspicions that it was built with the fines extracted from colliers who were absent from work on Mondays.

With the financial success of the Manchester canal, a lot of the Duke's personal spending restrictions eased. He, too, joined the house builders and erected a new hall, in classical style, to the south of the old half-timbered hall. Known as the Red Brick Hall, it was completed in 1768. The Gilberts went to live there, leaving the old hall as offices for the growing concern, and the Duke lodged there during his infrequent visits to Worsley.

Methods of reaching potential recruits for the workforce were many, but on being hired, all were under a contract to serve for a set period. This system, known as bonding, became widely used in Lancashire. Enticed by ale or cash offers, the collier signed an agreement to work, usually for a year. Men frequently deserted and the records show expenses incurred in 'seeking and fetching back colliers who had deserted the works'. Desertions appear to have occurred in spates, presumably when other, more congenial work was to be had. At one time 76 colliers, craftsmen and labourers received a two-and-a-half pence bonus, 'being retained not to desert his graces works without giving six months notice'. Persistent offenders there were: when they were looking for one collier so that he could be charged with the expenses of finding him, it was reported to the colliery agent that 'he is not now in his Grace's works, he having deserted again'. The

The Barracks cottages and bridge over the mineral railway. These were to the north of what is now Ashton Field Drive

continued use of ale as an inducement is evident from the accounts, a typical entry being 'paid for ale for treating Worsley and Dixon Green colliers £15.12.'

Once he was hired and had started work, the collier received his wages monthly. This meant there was great reliance on the use of the canteen or 'tommy shop', where goods could be had on credit and deductions were made for them before the next wages were paid. Control was exercised over the shops on the estate, the keepers being tenants at will: only household needs were permitted on credit and alcohol was prohibited. This truck system as applied at Worsley was praised in a contemporary report on social conditions. It says 'By such methods the collier always has credit for such necessities, and reasonable comforts'. The report also indicates that the Worsley wages were low on average, but this was offset by low-rent tied housing, cottage rents being 50p per year. Domestic economics fluctuated widely between plenty and penury and it was noted that when first the wages were paid, the collier and his family might indulge in meat foods three times a day. The week after, it is true, they had to descend to rye bread with oatmeal and water until the next wages were paid.

Treacle Row on Manchester Road East, Little Hulton. Typical miners' cottages of the Duke's estate

Methods of payment for work in the collieries did vary. Craftsmen, some direct labourers such as boatmen in the levels, and colliers in some districts were paid as daywagemen. Most of the colliers were paid piece rates. The bulk of the development work in driving the levels and shaft sinking was subcontracted. By this method, a 'butty' or ganger negotiated a piece rate with the mines agent and paid his own men. The work did have its benevolent side, with protective clothing issued to those working in difficult and exposed positions, and small gratuities eased the lot of those employees who became ill or disabled. Changes in terms of employment came gradually; use of the bond decreased and eventually ceased altogether in the early nineteenth century. Colliers were then hired or worked regularly by the fortnight, a certain amount of mobility of labour occurring in the slightly more varied local economy.

By the time the Duke's industries

The Duke's Brick Hall, Worsley. It was demolished in 1846

had become established, it is evident that conditions had improved on previous generations. Better housing, regular wages and an influx of people from other areas used to better things brought about many changes. Although the labour market had to take what it could get, the encouragement of promotion would be given to the more 'sober and dilligent'. Under the direction of the Gilberts, a sick club started, providing medical insurance for a subscription of ten pence per quarter year, and most employees became members. Educational needs were met by Sunday classes in private houses, a function largely transferred to the various religious bodies on their introduction to the district in the early nineteenth century.

Throughout the Duke's time, and later, the relief of the poor was the responsibility of the civil parish based on Eccles parish church. As the major local landowner, the estate contributed heavily to the funds for poor relief and these funds were especially useful to the colliers in the occasional depressions of trade in the first quarter of the nineteenth century.

As previously noted, it was the regular practice to employ virtually the whole family in the collieries and this practice, based on the labour intensive methods in use, continued at Worsley until about 1840. A rigid hierarchy of job grades grew up around the system, with adult males hewing the coal and women and youths

Colliers about 1840 using riddles to avoid small coal, an unsaleable product

transporting it underground. Small children were used as their physique determined, assisting their elders at repetitive tasks.

That there was official recognition of the status of workers dependent on age and sex is indicated by the customary grade scale in use at Worsley, the basis of which was the work output of an adult male. This output could be divided into eight parts and the general scale was:

Children:	one eighth
at 10 years:	two eighths
at 13 years:	three eighths
at 15 years:	one half
girls at 16:	one half
boys at 18:	three quarters

At that age boys began to get coal. Girls and women rarely got coal, and so remained haulage workers. The wages could vary considerably with seasonal and trade fluctuations, the rate for an adult male being in the range of two to four pounds per month.

With the precedent of family labour in agriculture, it is hardly surprising that it should continue in collieries. The lack of suitable alternative employment in the rather isolated Worsley community would also be a factor in retaining the custom. It was not until the 1850s that any real alternatives in textile mills were available within easy reach of Worsley.

The question of the employment of females and children underground is very often over-emphasised, particularly when the ratio of such workers is examined. From a total colliery employment roll of 1,600 persons, the ratio of workers was:-

Adults over 21 years:	965 male
	50 female
Aged 13 to 18 years:	322 male
	75 female
Aged under 13 years:	172 male
	20 female

Admittedly these figures were obtained in 1840, when a serious attempt was being made locally to tackle the worst abuses of female and child labour, but it is likely that they were fairly typical of the preceding half century.

A collier undercutting the coal. The hardest and most responsible job in the pits

Coal getters and coal drawers

After John Gilbert's initial technical improvements had been implemented, there were few major changes before about 1840. There was some adoption of steam for coal winding and pumping water. In addition, some of the methods in use from the earlier years became more extensively used as the principles behind their application were better understood.

The collieries of the Duke's time, and of the early years of the Trust, fell into two distinct groups which developed technically out of phase with each other. The main group numerically comprised those pits

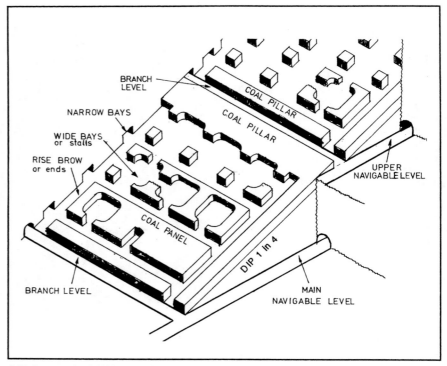

Mining method 1760-1850

based on the great Level, and which relied upon it for transport of coal and supplies. It also furnished their drainage and the bulk of their ventilation. The second group was the most important from a technical point of view. These pits developed independently of the Level, and relied completely on shafts for their services. They were the proving ground for mining engineering at Worsley. Since the most up-to-date methods had to be applied to make them function economically, it was usually the case that any innovation in the district appeared at these pits first.

As producers of coal for a competitive market, both the Duke's agents and their successors in the Trust applied the latest advances in mining science where they could be usefully employed. Perhaps the difference was that the Duke's staff were natural innovators, whilst the corporate structure of the Trust was intrinsically more cautious. Yet the Trustees, too, were forced to introduce new methods to keep abreast in a commercial world.

Winning of coal from the ground takes place in two distinct operations; reaching the coal and then extracting it. The usual method of reaching coal is by a vertical shaft through the overlying strata. Worsley used

several methods of access: shafts in plenty, sloping adits or 'day eyes', and the horizontal great Navigable Level.

Where access to the coal was concerned, the direction of advance was largely immaterial; in the early days the same technique was used, whether horizontal or vertical. A small team of tunnel miners or shaft sinkers would be employed and having first cleared surface deposits and exposed the rock, they would begin blasting. Using a star drill and sledge hammers, known locally as hammer chompers, a series of holes would be drilled about a yard deep. These were cleared of debris with a long spoon and partly filled with black gunpowder. A clay plug was then pressed in, a hole pricked through and a fuse, usually a straw filled with fine gunpowder, inserted. After firing, the rubble had to be removed by hand, and then the process was repeated. It is very doubtful if advances of more than a yard a day were achieved, particularly at greater depths where there was water to contend with as well.

The debris, with any accumulation of water, was removed from shafts by means of a kibble or bucket, hoisted by a horse gin. Ventilation to sinkings was poorly attended to; a crude hand bellows was the best that could be hoped for. A few

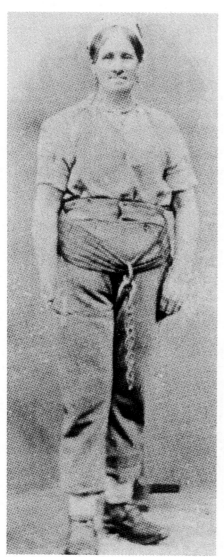

Mary Whittaker of Walkden, photographed about 1870 wearing the pit clothes and drawing belt and chain which she had worn as a girl in Edgefold Pit

shafts even remained unlined, although most of the shafts intended for permanent use had brick linings. The bricklayers worked higher up the shaft than the sinkers. As bricks have to be laid upwards from a solid base, a groove would be cut around the shaft and a wooden curb fitted. Brickwork could then be coursed up to meet the previous curb.

By modern standards the shafts sunk during this early period were only very shallow; those needing to reach the Level varied from thirty feet deep at Worsley to about a hundred feet at Walkden. The sheer number of such shafts is an indication of the labour that went into their construction. Initially designed with economy of effort in mind, the early shafts were often as small as six feet in diameter. With the realisation that winding would have to be used, particularly at the pits independent of the Level, a mean of ten to twelve feet became the norm. This size left room for the winding gear, and there was perhaps a slightly smaller shaft for pumping and to assist ventilation.

On reaching the coal by whatever method, work could start on extraction. The drawing reproduced on page 26 will perhaps make the system used a little easier to understand. The

Brick arches at Brassey Seam Branch, Parr Fold

method is generally known as pillar and stall; longwall working was not unknown in this period, but it was introduced more widely in later years. From the lowest point reached in the seam, a way would be cut at right angles to the dip to form either the branch level or a haulage road. Branch waterways were made with the roof of the seam forming the roof of the level, the water channel being cut in the lower rock strata.

Owing to the prolonged use of the lower main road in shaft-based pits, these too would be extended beyond the thickness of the seam. Timber props or brick walling with timber roof bars would be used in supporting these roadways.

Working 'ends' or rise brows up the incline of the seam were then cut at about 80 yard intervals. These extended up the seam as far as possible. Often a small ventilation shaft would be made at the upper end. The resulting panel of coal would then be further sub-divided by narrow cross passages, to leave smaller cross panels of coal about 15 yards thick on the rise. All these preliminary works were narrow, usually four to five feet wide, with the object of making them largely self-supporting. A further economy was to make them only the height of the seam, avoiding any expense for dead work in cutting rock.

The work of cutting the stalls to extract the coal fully could begin at this stage. The operation invariably started at the point furthest away from the shaft or branch level, so as progressively to reduce the distance the coal had to be hauled. Starting with narrow entrances in the cross ribs, the stalls were gradually widened up the dip, until adjacent stalls almost merged. Roof supports of timber props were used in these stalls or wide

Testing for gas in the Worsley seam, 222 feet below ground. The workings are still self-supporting

bays. After the full 15 yards panel had been so worked, most of the pillars would be removed and the props withdrawn, allowing the worked-out section to collapse. Often the end pillars were left to maintain an air passage in the working end. Support panels were also left on the rise side of each branch level. These 20-yard thick supports were often removed before the final abandonment of a branch. A similar unworked band would be left to protect any workings of the same seam at the deeper level.

In these days of coal cutting machines with huge outputs, the work of colliers using hand tools is often underestimated. The coal getter was always acclaimed as the élite of the pit's labour force. His job, by nature physically gruelling, was also one of the most dangerous. Each seam worked had geological features that determined the method used to cut the coal. This often took advantage of small bands of dirt within the thickness of the seam, or chose a weaker floor or roof material as an easier place to use the pick.

Whilst lying on his side, the collier

A branch level cut through rock to the first Three Quarters Seam below the Cock Hotel, Worsley

undercut the coal seam as deeply as possible, usually three to four feet. The groove so cut tapered from front to back for 'elbow room', the back being just the thickness of the pick head. A good collier would cut a length of from five to seven yards in this manner per shift. The coal then had to be parted from the roof with wedges. In more obstinate coal, shotholes would have to be drilled by hand and fired. Small props or chocks protected the collier whilst he was cutting the groove. A sharp pick was essential and the usual collier's equipment consisted of a handle and several heads, these being changed as they blunted during the shift. Pick heads went to the blacksmith for sharpening when they were really worn.

Great economy in the use of timber supports in any of the workings was a notable feature and self-supporting roadways, or brickwork linings in permanent roads, appear to have been normal practice. Yet despite sparing use and salvage, in a concern the size of these pits, large quantities of props had to be supplied. According to the records, once the local woods had been exhausted the districts of Ringley and Clifton became prime suppliers.

The canal under Walkden at Deborah Pillar Junction. These magnificent brick arches support the Seven Feet Seam branch on the right, which went to Berry Field. Although over two hundred years old, the brickwork appears to be in remarkably good condition. The craftsmanship of the bricklayers, working by candlelight in dangerous and unpleasant conditions, is clearly evident

The only treatment that coal received as regards preparation for market was done by the collier. He was responsible for removing any dirt or shale before the coal was sent out. Any small coal had to be riddled underground to remove the fines and the yard depot sold the colliers sieves for this purpose.

Until the mid-1840s most hewn coal was moved by very primitive means. Wicker baskets or wooden boxes with iron-shod sledge runners underneath were stacked with lump coal, or filled with riddled pieces. They would then have to be dragged along the mine floor to the shaft or boat and it was this work, usually performed by women and children, that caused a national outcry when revealed by a Royal Commission in 1842.

All the work done by these human pit ponies had to be on hands and knees or at a crawl in the low passages, and this when the laden sledges weighed from two to four hundredweight. The leader, termed a drawer, wore a broad belt with a short chain and hook attached. This passed between the legs to the sledge. At the rear, one or two children pushed or 'thrutched' the load. Quite phenomenal feats of endurance were regularly undertaken by these drawers, as the records of the Commission's report show. Commenting on workers at the Worsley collieries, it quotes an interview with a 16-year-old girl:
'How long have you been in the pits?'
'I have been four years in the pits. I am a drawer and work for my father.'
'What hours do you work?'
'Sometimes I come at five o'clock in the morning, sometimes six and seven; and I go up at three, four, five and six o'clock at night, just as it happens.'
'What distance do you draw?'
'180 yards, 10 or 12 times a day, sometimes more and sometimes less, just as it happens.' [Allowing for the return journey, this adds up to a distance of some two-and-a-half miles.]
'Do you draw with a belt and chain?'
'Yes.'
'Have you wheels to your tubs?'
'No; we sled 'em.'

In an interview with an engineer at another local pit:
'What is the greatest distance you have known a drawer travel in one day?'
'I have known a drawer travel 700 yards each way on the level, with

rails, 10 times. 225 yards up brow, without rails, 20 times a-day, belt and chain. And 30 yards without rails on the level with belt and chain each way 20 times. This in a day of 14 to 15 hours.' [A total distance of thirteen-and-three-quarter miles - made possible by the use of rails for most of the day.]

These rails were a welcome introduction at some pits. They consisted of flat plates with guide flanges and the wheeled basket tubs could be hauled two at a time by the drawers. A further refinement was the use of jig brows, or smaller versions of the inclined plane, lowering tubs instead of boats. Few actual ponies were used underground before the 1840s. The only place likely to have used them was the main connecting tunnel, or wagon road as it was always called, from the Roe Green workings to the Level at Kempnough.

All this work underground both at the face and in the roadways took place by candlelight; in the pre-safety-lamp days there was no real alternative to candles or oil lamps. The colliers' candles were small wax dips, weighing about 24 to the pound, and six or more would be used per shift. A distinctive feature

of these candles was the greeny-coloured flame caused by the arsenic in them - it was said the arsenic reduced a candle's tendency to gutter in the draughts of the mine.

It was in the shafts and the services they supplied that changes in technology really appeared. The interrelated functions of winding and pumping were gradually undertaken by steam power.

Most of the shafts serving the branches of the Navigable Level were used only for personnel and occasional services, hence ladders and some horse gins continued in use throughout the active life of the branch. The free drainage provided by the main Level led to water-balance winding being retained at major shafts connecting the lower to the main Levels until the mid-nineteenth century. In operation, the headframe held two rope drums separated by a larger brake pulley. One rope went down to the lower Level to take the coal tub, the other had a water tub attached at the surface. When filled and the brake released, the heavier water tub drew up the coal tub, the pulleys being arranged so that both tubs reached the main Level together, where the water was discharged and the coal removed

A clow, or sluice, used to control the water level and flush boats along tunnels of the Navigable Level

using another device. As the shafts were some yards from the waterway, a machine had been developed to aid the movement. A tramway ran across the shaft to the Level. On this ran a trolley on to which the loaded tub was lowered by the water engine. Uncoupled from the rope, it was then pushed to the Level for emptying.

Determining just when and where steam was first introduced to the Worsley mines poses many problems. The term 'engine' was used for virtually any mechanical contrivance, as was its contraction, 'gin'. Further confusion is caused by many of the early steam engines having the dual function of pumping and winding, enhanced rates being paid for pumping at night at pits so equipped. Cookes Meadow pits at Abbots Fold had a steam gin as early as 1771, most likely just for pumping, whilst a further engine was installed in 1798, almost certainly for winding. The pits at Dixon Green also had a steam engine installed in 1771.

In the first quarter of the nineteenth century most of the new sinkings were provided with steam power. These engines were of small capacity, 10hp being about average. Surprisingly, considering the wide use of the balanced load principle (as in the inclined plane and water-balance winding), most of the early steam winders worked on direct haulage. To avoid overstraining the engines, many forms of variable gearing were tried. Among the most successful of these were tapered drums, with the wind starting at the small end. Alternatively, flat ropes were used, consisting of small cables laid side-by-side and sewn together to form what looked like a long belt. When this was wound on to a drum in the manner of a clock spring, the ever altering diameter varied the load on the engine. Both of these methods remained in use at a few of the pits originally fitted with them until late in the nineteenth century.

Hemp ropes were widely used for winding purposes for want of anything better, the first iron wire rope being bought in 1819. Unfortunately where it was used is not recorded. No doubt expense went against their immediate adoption at all pits, despite the fact that rope breakages were frequent and feature regularly in accident reports of the time. The root cause appears to have been almost complete indifference by the engineers to the state of the ropes. The previously quoted government report of 1842 brings out this point in some of its interviews. A local winding engineer was questioned:
'Were the ropes always kept in good order?'
'The ropes in some places were bad, and in others better... I have known a rope break; nobody was killed or lamed; the rope was a very bad one; it was pieced with iron couplings in several places, and in many parts of the rope one or two of the strands were broken.'
'Was there any time fixed for the renewing of the ropes?'
'When the rope was out of repair the men complained to the engineer, and the engineer mentioned it to the underlooker.'

Another collier tells much the same story:

'At the Duke's they have made a change lately; formerly the men never knew when they were to have a new rope till it came, and they had to couple it five or six times before they got a new one, and sometimes they used to wear nine or ten years without a new one.'

Winding speeds were necessarily slow to keep control of the freely swinging baskets being hoisted. The introduction of guides for the loads in the shaft, initially timber baulks secured to the lining, allowed an increase in speed up to about 10 feet per second. The fitting of guides was justified only at some of the independent pits and several had been installed by 1825. Unfortunately the accident toll continued at pits not so fitted, with free-swinging baskets catching on the side and discharging their contents, human or mineral. This state of affairs continued until the early 1840s.

As previously described, the Navigable Level was designed to

A starvationer 'T' boat in dry dock, showing the rugged construction

overcome most of the drainage problems of the districts it served. However, regular working took place at a greater depth than was served by gravity discharge and this led to the introduction of a device for using the deadweight of water for pumping. It was described by Sir Joseph Banks on his visit in 1765: 'In the lower levels of parts of these works they are obliged to lift water, and have devised an engine for that purpose. The weight of a column of water thrown down a shaft is made to lift a piston which works two lifts of pumps.' It was, in fact, a water-balance pump which, according to the detailed sketch in Banks' report, had been made self-acting with trip valves.

In principle, the weight of the pump rods running down the shaft depressed the plunger and primed the pump barrel. A counterbalance tank then filled with water, lifting the plunger and the mine water. At the end of the stroke, both the mine and balance water were discharged into the Level. Two lifts of pumps were often needed to span the height between the sump and the discharge outlet. This machine, like a number of the devices peculiar to the workings of the Worsley mines, was the work of a Mr Ashton Tonge, a millwright turned mine engineer, brought to Worsley for his expertise by John Gilbert.

The development of steam engines

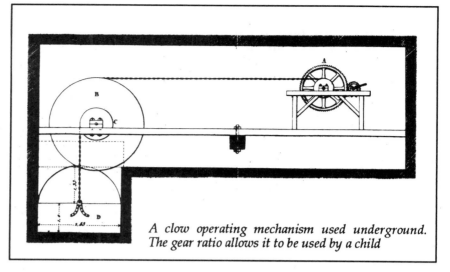

A clow operating mechanism used underground. The gear ratio allows it to be used by a child

specifically for mine drainage is a well documented story and it is certain that use was made of them at Worsley from the 1770s. Initially of low horsepower and always of low speed, these engines were usually reliable and equal to their work. In operation, the cylinder and beam depressed and raised a pump rod which was about eight inches square and ran the full depth of the shaft; these timber 'rods' running in guides on the shaft wall operated the pump plunger.

Steam pumps of this type were a feature of pits independent of the Level, and the rate of installation appears to have kept pace with new sinkings and deep development. So small were these early engines that it was normal practice to move them around to

several pits during the engine's working life. Even the engine from the successful, but aborted, attempt at a steam-powered boat at Worsley in 1795 ended its days powering a colliery pump. Of the dozen or so pumping engines in use by the close of the century, 20hp was about the average size, though some of the new sinkings by the Trustees in the 1820s had pumps of up to 70hp installed.

Ventilation of the workings also received its due share of improvements in these formative years. Although the Duke's pits were not troubled to the same extent with gas as some other coalfields, enough was present to make the work hazardous, and in the extended Worsley pits even supplying sufficient air for breathing often posed problems.

Those pits on the Navigable Level could to a certain extent rely upon the natural current of air set in motion by temperature changes. Normally the warmer air in the pit rose out through one of the many access or air shafts, drawing in air through the Level mouth at Worsley. Unfortunately, however, high summer temperatures would upset this air flow, often even reversing it. One of the earlier sources of forced ventilation at the Navigable Level pits used the power of falling water. A magazine of 1763 described its operation:

'At the mouth of the cavern is erected a water bellows, being the body of a tree forming a hollow cylinder standing upright. Upon this, a wooden basin is fixed in the form of a funnel which receives a

A collier undercutting a wide lift of coal with very sparing use of timber supports. A typical pre-1860 scene

current of water from the higher ground. This water falls into the cylinder and issues out at the bottom of it. But at the same time carries a quantity of air with it which is received into tin pipes and forced into the enormous recesses of the coal pits.'

The independent pits could not obtain this advantage, and soon passed the stage where bellows and hand fans were of any use. Many coalfields had experimented with the use of firebaskets or furnaces in a shaft, so the warmed air would induce an air current, and Worsley soon adopted the idea. In 1769 a shaft at Edgefold was called the Firepit and judging by the quantity of coal consumed there, it must have had a form of ventilating furnace. By 1771 the Abbots Fold pits had 'damp fires' charged as using coal and under this very descriptive name furnaces can be traced at many more of the early pits, being a relatively inexpensive solution to a major problem.

Initially, a firebasket was placed at the top of the shaft, but its efficiency was much improved by putting it at the bottom in a well-made brick structure. Later, with multiple fire holes, these furnaces became the standard ventilating

force at pits until the late 1860s. Surprisingly few accidents occurred through having such large fires underground.

Once a ventilating draught had been created, means were provided to direct the air into the places where work was going on. Doors were erected at intersections to direct the air and young children were employed to keep them closed after the passage of tubs. Dead end headings were ventilated by hanging cloth down the centre so that a two-way air flow could be introduced. Many entries in the accounts record buying 'cloth to turn the air' and early engravings of the Level entrance show ventilation doors fitted.

Despite these improvements, prudent colliers always checked for gas before starting work. A record of the type of trial commonly used is given in Thomas Bury's notes in 1778: 'If the flame spires up and begins to lift, it is an infallible rule it is going to fire. Again if the flame be broad at the top and bright, begins to spurt out at all sides, then it is certain that you are far enough, for it will fire almost immediately.'

That frequent firing of the gas did

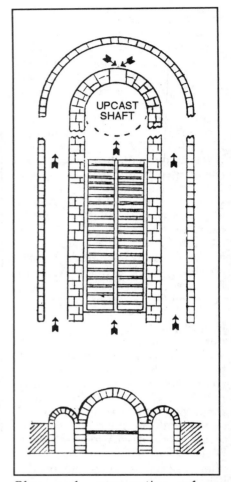

Plan and cross-section of an underground ventilating furnace, used at the bottom of shafts until prohibited in 1911

occur is shown by the account entries for the regular purchase of 'Extract of Saturn' to treat the colliers burned in the pit, this medicament being bought in 14lb jars. Well over 50% of total accidents recorded in the Trustees' accident ledger were caused by fire-damp explosions and most resulted in injury to several people.

The most outstanding technical achievement at Worsley was obviously the underground Navigable Level. Whilst not unique, it was almost certainly the first of its kind. Others were developed by mineral owners who were friends of the Duke, and elsewhere, but the features that put the Worsley Navigable Level at the forefront of achievements were its extent and its durability. There were over 50 miles of tunnels navigable by loaded boats; the Level served its prime function of transporting coal for 125 years and it had a useful life of over 200 years.

A 'fireman' clearing out gas by igniting it, as practised in the early days of coal mining

Whilst serving an active extraction industry, the layout of the Level was constantly changing. Branches and whole districts were abandoned when worked out, whilst extensions were in hand at other places.

The methods used to drive most of the Level had hardly changed from the days of cutting the soughs. Apart from direction, they were little different from shaft sinking; star drills, hammers and gunpowder were virtually the only equipment employed by the small rock mining teams. The new heading face would be separated from the completed waterway by a clay dam, behind which boats received the spoil from the tunnellers. One of the most notable aspects of the construction is the marvellous way in which the brick arches were built. These supported the tunnel through less stable strata and in spite of the ground pressure they stood with little maintenance until the final abandonment. Some intersections with branches to east and west made arches up to sixteen feet wide, with in no instance any support other than keying in the brickwork to the rock. The photographs on page 28 show the difference between the arched and unlined sections of tunnel.

The boats in use on these levels were purpose-built with many specially adapted features. Once taken into a tunnel they could not be turned round, so both ends were shaped as bows for travelling in either direction. Rudely finished, but of sound construction to withstand hard usage, their internal appearance earned their nickname of 'starvationers'. The ribs which rose from a flat bottom to support the vertical sides were uncovered, giving them a very hungry look.

There were three distinct sizes of boats in use. The largest, used only on the main Level, was 53 feet long, 6 feet beam, and carried up to 10 tons of coal. Unloaded, these drew only 8 inches of water and when full, some 28 inches of the boat's 34-inch depth. Largely intended for use on the side branches and on the upper Levels were smaller boats of 7 or 8 tons capacity, 50 feet long, 4 feet 6 inches beam and 30 inches deep. All these boats had access to the boatyard at Worsley for major repairs. Minor running repairs were done underground by the yard carpenters.

However, to get boats into any of the lower levels meant they had to be lowered vertically down a shaft, and to make this easier shafts serving the lower levels were often made elliptical, or were bellied out at the bottom. Certainly the boats used in these lower levels were smaller than the others - they were only 30 feet long and 4 feet beam, and carried only 2 tons.

Each boat had a fleet number and a code letter to indicate its type. The 10-ton boats were M or mine boats, whilst the 7-tonners were known as T boats. The small boats on the lower levels were unlettered but called Tub boats. Generally all the loaded M boats and some of the T boats were hauled directly to Manchester from the Level entrance. Contents of other T boats would be transferred to other boats at the Delph basin, and eventually all the boats would be returned underground. The approximate size of the fleet in 1840 was 75 each of the M and T boats, with 100 small Tub boats. The size and composition of the fleet would alter with changes in the use of the Levels in later years.

The boats were usually drawn along the trunk main Level in groups of 6 to 10. There are exaggerated stories of people managing huge fleets of up to 70 boats, but the sheer impracticality of this is obvious. Apart from being half the total stock of boats, such a fleet would be 1,200 yards long - stretching from the canal to the East Lancashire Road. The transfer basin at the entrance could only hold about 30 boats, another useful pointer to the usual train size.

Each of the pits or branch Levels had a group of boatmen responsible for movement of full and empty boats. This was no easy job, just sailing up and down all day. It was reckoned that the trip from the Dean Moor pits took five hours each way. Generally the boatmen considered it slavish work. 'Strong i'th' arm and weak i'th' head is what's wanted here,' is the recorded comment of one of them. Methods of moving the empty boats into the Levels changed over the years. Originally, whilst at work each man had on a harness or sling of broad canvas to which was attached some six feet of rope terminating in a hook. Standing at the front of the first boat and facing the direction of progress, the boatman would hook himself to a staple inserted in the roof. (The staples were some ten feet apart.) He would pass the boat under his feet, unhook, and return to the front end to repeat the

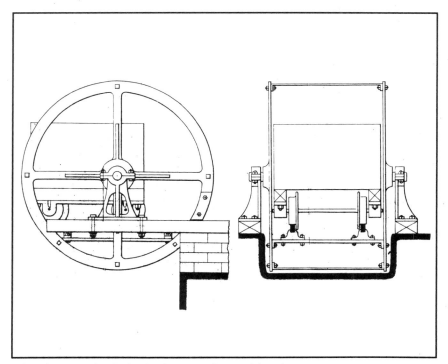

A hand-operated tub tippler for emptying coal into boats

process. By the 1840s, perhaps because of smaller tunnels or because of silting, the method had changed to legging. The men lay on their backs on a bench at the end of the boat and moved it by walking their feet along the roof of the tunnel.

The loaded boats were brought out of the Level more easily than empty ones were taken into it. At intervals are clows, or sluice gates, which cause the water to rise, on the inward side, from six inches to a foot higher than on the outward side. These sluices had a windlass set into a side chamber which lifted the gate into a recess in the roof and clear of the arch. When a train of loaded boats was approaching, the gate was raised and the flow of water carried them to the next lock, and so on until daylight was reached. Once the loaded boats had gone and the wave subsided, the empty boats could go up. At intervals along the trunk levels there were 'wides', or

lay-bys, where the Level was 14 to 20 feet wide. These were for storing boats or allowing fleets to pass and they varied in length from 50 to 350 feet.

Methods of loading these boats varied according to the Level where they were in use. On the deep Levels, the coal was transferred from the sledges into barrel-like tubs complete with lifting lugs, and holding about 6 cwt. Six of these fitted into the spaces between the ribs of the tub boats. On the Main and Upper Levels coal was often tipped directly into the boat. At the loading point, platforms known as teeming stages ran above the boat and were fitted with counterbalanced tipplers. These discharged the coal from the sledges (or, later, wheeled tubs) into the boat. At some places the coal was tipped down a small shaft or teeming hole into a waiting boat. Increased use was made of 'containerisation' on all Levels in

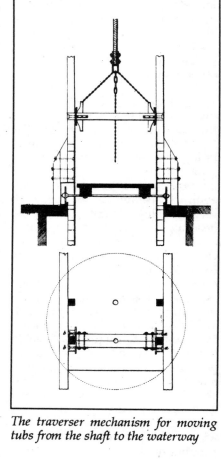

The traverser mechanism for moving tubs from the shaft to the waterway

later years: these rectangular boxes eased movement of coal at all points in its journey from the drawer's sledge to the consumer.

The production of individual colliers - they were paid on output - could be separated by stop planks across the width of the boat against the ribs, or restricted to individual boxes. The contents of the boats were checked for weight against gauge lines marked on the sides, the water level indicating how heavy they were.

A few statistics will help to bring the work of the collieries and particularly the haulage of coal into perspective. For a long period, the output through the Level was 100,000 tons per year or more. This averages 2,000 tons per week, involving dealing with some 40 boats per day at the Worsley Delph basin. Underground, over 2,500 sledge or tub loads would be hauled by the drawers per working day.

The chart (Appendix 4) gives some idea of the equipment in use by 1840, and the size of the labour force at the various collieries or Levels.

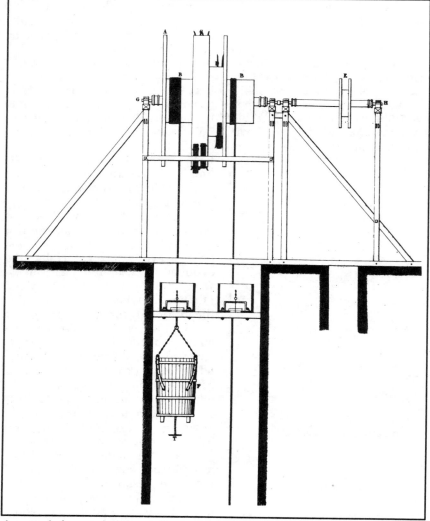

A water-balance winding mechanism and brake system

Under the Duke's Will

On the death of the Duke, his will laid out the provisions for the future of the estates and undertakings. The landed estates or non-industrial side went to the issue of his uncle, the Bishop of Hereford. This was the Bishop's son, John Egerton, who also became the seventh Earl of Bridgewater. The Worsley estates and the canal interests passed under a Trust to the issue of the Duke's sister, Lady Louisa Egerton, wife of the second Earl Gower. The beneficiary was George Leveson Gower, the Marquis of Stafford. Under the terms of the Duke's remarkable will, Lord Stafford did not gain complete possession of the concern, but was merely to draw the profit from it as income, without any executive power.

The industrial enterprise, which included the collieries, was to be vested in a Trusteeship. This was to be directed by a body of three Trustees with one, the superintendent, having almost dictatorial powers. The Trust, the Duke decreed, was to last for the lives of all the peers of the kingdom, and certain relatives of the Duke, and for a further twenty years. It continued, despite many inherent disadvantages and with many changes of personnel and policy, for its allotted time. In fact it ran for exactly one hundred years.

In separating the beneficiary from any control, it is possible that the Duke intended to prevent the Staffords, who had their own coal and canal interests, from showing preference to their own estates. The whole Trust had to conform to the testament of the Duke, whatever action was needed or crisis met, and this did lead to administrative problems in later years, when events came about that the Duke could not have foreseen. Markets for coal changed and transport systems altered with the coming of the railways. Changes were inevitable and many were the devices used to implement them.

As originally convened in 1803, the Bridgewater Trust had as members the then Chancellor of the Exchequer, Sir A Macdonald; the Bishop of Carlisle, Edward Harcourt and, as superintendent, Robert Haldane Bradshaw. The superintendent had the executive power of the concern in all its branches, meriting a salary of £2,000 per annum, together with the use of the Red Brick Hall at Worsley. To ensure consistent direction of the enterprise, under the terms of the will the superintendent had the power to nominate his successor.

Robert Haldane Bradshaw, the eldest son of the secretary to the Treasury, was born in 1759. He entered public service and eventually became an agent for the Duke. In fact, he took over the duties of Thomas Gilbert as legal agent centred on Bridgewater House in London. He was also M.P. for the Duke's pocket borough of Brackley in Northamptonshire from 1802 until 1832. Bradshaw moved to Worsley in 1810, taking a further interest in local affairs by becoming a magistrate for the district.

Opinions of Bradshaw as a Trustee vary. Some saw him as a hard-headed businessman whose main aim was profit and who was responsible for many of the social evils of the time. Others paint a more sympathetic picture. Taking into account the restrictions placed on him by the terms of the Duke's will, the more favourable view is probably nearer the truth - Bradshaw tried to keep his employees in work even in bad times. It is likely that his main faults were due to his character: reluctant to delegate and intensely conservative, he was eventually out of his depth with the responsibility and rapidly changing economic circumstances.

In such a widespread enterprise, stretching from Worsley to Runcorn on the Mersey and to Castlefield in Manchester, some delegation there had to be. In those days before the telephone, a reliable person on the spot was invaluable. The new superintendent made use of the existing management structure, with Benjamin Sothern remaining as principal agent. Under Sothern, heads of departments known variously as agents or inspectors controlled the different sections of the concern.

The inspector in charge of the collieries was Moses Bury, who held the post until 1828. The position was then taken by John

The Works Yard at Worsley, now 'The Green'. The clock struck thirteen at one o'clock

Ridyard, who received promotion to mines agent in 1837 and appointed his son James as his assistant. Another son, Thomas, became colliery engineer and several other members of the family were also employed at the collieries. In the aftermath of the Trust's upheavals related in the next chapter, changes were made between 1838 and 1840. John Pickup became colliery agent, with Ridyards as viewer and assistant. Later, William Denby was engaged as coal solicitor and Daniel Timmins as colliery engineer, but the Ridyards retained senior positions throughout the period of the Trust.

Individual collieries were supervised by banksmen and underlookers, officers who were in charge of individual pits or branch seams of the Navigable Level, and answerable to the viewer or mines agent. It would appear that the underground layout of the collieries with regard to overcoming geological problems and distributing the working faces was in the hands of the viewer. The engineer was mainly responsible for the installation and maintenance of mechanical plant, winding and pumping units, a staff and facilities being maintained at Worsley and Walkden yards for the purpose.

This was still before the railways, when the output of the collieries depended upon local market forces and the ability of the Trust to satisfy the demand. Within the stranglehold of limited investment decreed by the Duke's will, not all the advances that could have been

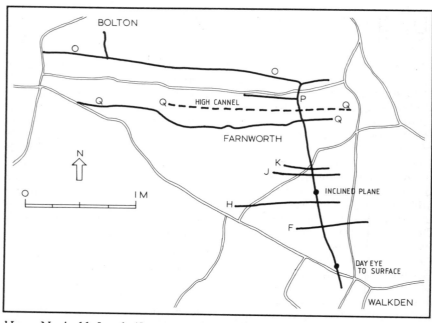

Upper Navigable Levels (See seam sequence chart, page 2)

made were achieved. Internal inefficiency also helped to minimise what expansion there was in this period.

During the Duke's lifetime, the colliery output had risen fairly steadily to a peak of about 140,000 tons per year by 1800. After his death, output declined to about 99,000 tons in 1809. Thereafter the production figures, although fluctuating, show a general rise to 165,000 tons in 1830 and the 1830s saw almost a doubling of this output. By the end of the decade, the older workings along the Navigable Level were becoming exhausted. Recourse was had to the development of the east and west flanks of the Worsley coalfield with independent pits, a continuation of a policy begun in the 1820s with the deeper levels,

whose development will be outlined later in this chapter.

Within the first quarter of the nineteenth century the Upper Navigable Level had ceased to be a major coal producing unit. From its inception it had been known as the Walkden Moor section of the colliery. Following the swift advance of its axial waterway, its southerly arms were soon worked out and the east arm of the Black seam was abandoned in 1780. The west arm, which advanced slowly for its 1,200-yard length, lasted until 1798, while the twin arms of the Old Doe seam, each 400 yards long, had been discontinued by 1802.

The more valuable northerly seams were more extensively and speedily worked. The Cannel seam,

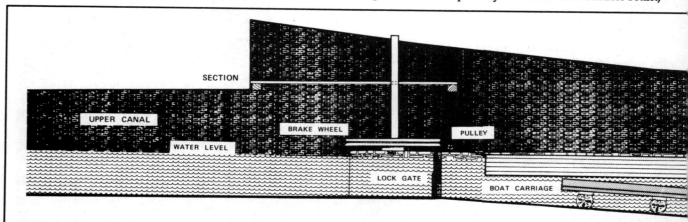

The mechanism of the Inclined Plane with the later brake wheel shown

intercepted 200 yards south of Highfield Road in 1780, had a rapid advance, its west arm being worked continuously until 1802, to a distance of 2,650 yards from the axial level. It was subsequently re-worked for a further 1,000 yards, in later years using boat haulage and shaft access through Watergate pit. A small advance was made in the Cannel seam to the west, but this was abandoned in 1794.

The Dean Moor seam, 200 yards north of Plodder Lane in Farnworth, was the most northerly reached and it was worked extensively westwards, despite many interruptions, often of several years' duration. Work stopped at 1,500 yards from 1795 until 1801. Further intermittent advances were made until its final length - some 4,300 yards, or nearly two-and-a-half miles - was reached. This level, the most extensive in the whole system, terminated to the west of St Helens Road, near Four Lane Ends in Bolton. A small east level was worked in this seam for 300 yards. Then in 1806 development started in the Plodder seam, which for some reason had been bypassed previously, possibly because its coal was not as valuable as that of its neighbours. A 900-yard-long west arm grew until discontinued in late 1809.

To exploit further the valuable Cannel seam, an independent navigable level was started above the higher Level. This was situated in between the old Cannel sough workings and those of the west

The entrance to the Chaddock Levels. Owing to subsidence it is now below the level of the Bridgewater Canal

branch of the Upper Navigable Level. Its main surface connection was Green Ashes Croft pit near Highfield. Work started in 1786 and progressed westwards for 1,200 yards until 1795. A subsequent eastwards extension passed through Lords Moss Pit at Dixon Green with shaft access to both navigable levels, and advanced a further 600 yards from there, a total length of 2,700 yards.

Only when the amount of work involved is considered do these figures for the lengths of the level branches become meaningful. Under the Trustees, most branch levels were still driven under contract by a gang of specialist tunnellers. An account book entry gives some idea of the specification of these levels and the work

undertaken. The last advances of the Doe seam in 1802 are recorded, when 60 yards of tunnel were let under contract to F Crowther & Co. This was to be 10 feet 8 inches wide and 8 feet 6 inches high. The higher side to the coal was to be bricked to a height of 2 feet 6 inches to hold in the coal, and this support had to be one brick breadth thick. On the lower, or south, side, the wall was one brick length thick, 5 feet 10 inches high and puddled at the back with clay. All the spoil was 'filled' or removed to the surface at Tub Engine pit. The work took 23 weeks and cost £84. A further 40 yards, identical to the first, was charged at £56 and took 15 weeks to complete.

It is evident that the whole Upper Navigable Level system had become worked out or uneconomic by about 1820. Whilst no further regular working took place, the main axial Level was not abandoned as its drainage function was too important. The connecting inclined plane had worked well, but at some date unknown its mechanism was reconstructed and the main brake wheel now ran on a vertical spindle placed centrally between the twin top locks, the whole structure being well braced to the side walls and roof of the chamber. As an indication that the Upper Level was not to be completely abandoned, the rails for the boat cradles on the inclined plane were re-laid as late as 1819.

The main Navigable Level had

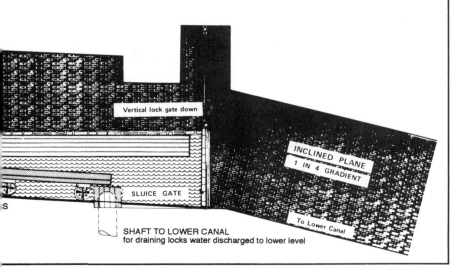

Vertical lock gate down

INCLINED PLANE 1 IN 4 GRADIENT

SLUICE GATE

To Lower Canal

SHAFT TO LOWER CANAL
for draining locks water discharged to lower level

progressed to Buckley Lane by 1801 but advances during the early nineteenth century were only intermittent. With the satisfactory rate of output from the Cannel seam in the Upper Level, it was probably not economic to extend the Main Level further until reserves in the latter were nearly worked out. It is also most likely that the relatively short branch levels in the belt of seams at Parr Fold in Walkden had been abandoned by this time.

The general outline of development appears to have been the extension of the existing branch levels south of Buckley Lane until about 1815, when it became apparent that the Upper Level would soon be worked out. In the next fifteen years, the Main Level having reached the Dean Moor seam, the bulk of the output came from these northern seams and the Boothstown development described later.

Of the seams north of the Barracks fault, the Windmill seam had a small west level driven, which continued under Worsley Road as work proceeded east. In the 1780s the twin Black and White seams were reached. A branch level was made in the Black seam and short tunnels to the south were driven to work the White seam coal from one waterway. The east level of this extended 560 yards to Worsley Road, whilst the west branch ran 1,220 yards to Cleggs Lane.

The second Doe seam intercepted in the late 1790s had branch levels on both flanks. To the east it was driven for 700 yards to the Buckley Lane fault, a move which threw the Black and White seams in line with these workings and where extraction continued. On the west flank, after 1,300 yards the multiple Buckley Lane faults were reached, stopping development. As a further economy of use, this long Doe level on both flanks was used to work the Five Quarters seam. Short, cross-measure level tunnels were driven north into this seam and the coal extracted by haulage roads to boats in the Doe level.

Work started in the Cannel seam from the main Navigable Level, and as it was now the main producer of this valuable fuel,

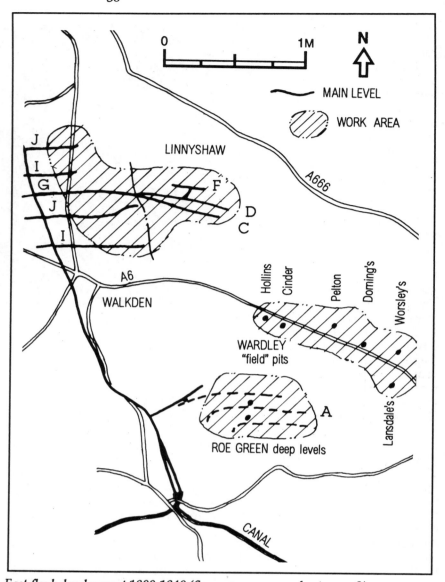

East flank development 1800-1840 (See seam sequence chart, page 2)

progress was rapid. As ever, the Main Level and its branch formed a bottleneck to boat traffic and to ease the situation a connection to the Old Doe workings was driven through the fault lines at 1,160 yards from the Main Level. These outlets for the loaded boats, still the most economic means of transport, allowed extension of the workings in the Cannel seam for up to 3,500 yards, reaching south of the A6 near Brackley.

The Plodder seam was indifferently worked for about 300 yards east and west at this period, though it was re-worked in later years by extending the level in the form of a wagon way. On the final advance of the Main Level to the Dean Moor seam, this arterial waterway reached 6,300 yards or three-and-a-half miles from Worsley. The seam was extensively worked - a distance of

1,100 yards was driven eastward and the branch level ran westward, closely following the line of Plodder Lane, for 3,800 yards nearly to St Helens Road.

More branches of the main Navigable Level were started in the early nineteenth century. The Windmill seam branch was extended from near the Barracks pit and under Hill Top. Part of the Buckley Lane fault was crossed and water transport access gained to a parcel of land owned by the Trustees north of Linnyshaw. Here lay the fourth series of the Binn, Croumbouke, Brassey and Seven Feet seams. Work had started on this series by 1818, and axial cross-measure tunnels joined the seams and used the Windmill seam level for transport. The workings were largely abandoned by 1835, but this system had waterways extending for over two miles during its working life, reckoned from its junction with the Windmill seam at the fault.

With the reduction of output potential from the Navigable Level in the early years of the Trust, the time was ripe for the development of other areas. As noted previously, the Duke had contracted many leases in the Boothstown and Tyldesley area. Undoubtedly these would have been worked, but to what extent is uncertain. After the Duke's death, the superintendent trustee, Robert Bradshaw, assisted in this expansion by buying land and leasing the coal to the Trust. In this way, the Booths Hall and Chaddock Hall estates were acquired in 1810 and the Garrett Hall estate in 1829. These lands gave good access to the Worsley Four Feet seam at an acceptable depth, while the completion of the surface canal through to Leigh provided adequate local transport facilities.

Movement of the coal to the canal was eased by duplicating the underground canal idea. Another navigable level was driven north from the canal near Boothsbank Bridge to intercept one of the principal pits of the district, Chaddock pit, sunk just south of Chaddock Lane. A further driving extended this level to the Queen Anne pit on Chaddock Lane, the total length being about 950 yards.

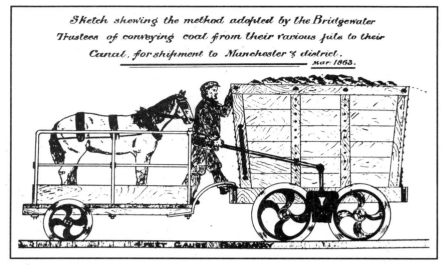

A tramway horse dolly

As the coal was deeper than the interception of the shafts with the new level, the method of working was similar to the operations on the deep levels at Worsley. From the shaft and seam intercept, navigable branch levels were driven and the coal worked to the rise and sledged to the level. At this point, the coal was loaded into tubs or boxes in the boats and floated to the shaft. It was then lifted up the shaft, transferred to boats in the Main Level and sailed to the canal.

Work on this development was well under way by 1819, when the level was being driven from the canal and Queen Anne pit was sunk. Chaddock pit, since it was

also needed for pumping the lower levels, had two shafts. One, the Pump or Engine pit, had a 70hp unit, the coal winding shaft managing with a 14hp engine; both were installed in 1820 into prepared engine houses. The entrance arch to the new level is inscribed '1822', its likely completion date.

Considerable advances were made in these deeper levels, paralleled in date by some in the same seam based on the Worsley level. Eventually the workings from Chaddock pit connected with those from the Wood pit deep levels, whilst those from the Queen Anne pit joined those from the Ingles pit. Both these connections gave an additional outlet to Worsley. Development also proceeded west from the Queen Anne pit in the form of a tunnel which crossed the Chaddock fault and provided water transport to the pits at Henfold. This whole system had a total extent of about three-and-a-half miles.

All this development contributed to the increased output of the 1830s, which appears to have been largely supplied by deeper workings. During the decade a significant number of these deeper levels of the navigable system were started or re-worked. The Barracks pit, for example, was deepened to work branch levels in the Black seam, whilst the range of multi-depth levels based on Edgefold pits was still being extended.

The canal at Worsley, with barge and coal boxes - an early form of containerisation

As a result either of the trade slump in the 1840s, or exhaustion of reserves, the workings based on the Chaddock level were largely abandoned by 1842. Most of the surface plant was then moved to other, still active districts, particularly Wardley, to the east of the Worsley coalfield.

As might be expected from a decade which saw a tremendous increase in coal output from fairly shallow reserves, the area worked had to be increased. The Boothstown development was not enough to meet demand, so new pits had to be sunk. The Navigable Level exploited a central corridor in the Trustees' Worsley coalfield. Now an attack was to be made on the flanks.

In the early 1820s minor sinkings had been made in Linnyshaw and Wardley and by the end of the decade about six pits worked the area. These collieries, substantial for the period, were dependent on steam for all shaft services. They were sited near the present A6 road through Wardley. Lansdales Field, Cinderfield, Worsleys and Dornings Field pits with Hollins Field pits formed this group, their names truly showing their intrusion into an agricultural district. All these pits worked the Worsley Four Feet, Binn and Croumbouke seams to the east of the Wardley fault. Some were to be redeveloped in later years, but this group had largely declined by the early 1860s.

A more important sinking took place at Sanderson's in Roe Green in the early 1830s, where a shaft worked the Four Feet seam. Whilst connections were made to the level-based workings in Roe Green, this pit relied on shaft services.

On the western flank, the area from Tynesbank and Hilton Lane south to Mosley Common started to be developed in a similar manner. The land at Common Head had been leased and work started. Pits were sunk at Burgess Land, Hilton Lane and Tynesbank, most of them destined to have long, productive lives.

Unfortunately, these pits suffered the disadvantage of having the transport cost added as an overhead at either the landsale or canal sale point. The Trust bowed

to the inevitable and, despite their opposition to 'national' railways, they started their own system. In reality these were tramways, horse drawn and single tracked. The accounts show in 1833: 'For forming a railway from Tynesbank pit to the canal near Boothsbank bridge, £125 this year.' Work continued in 1834 and 1835, being charged at £693 and £719 respectively, and was transferred to the east in 1835, when a similar tramway was made from Sanderson's to the canal near Worsley yard. This work was also spread over three years and cost £1,857 in total.

Both these tramways relied upon a falling gradient to assist in the movement of loaded wagons. The wagons ran on cast iron rails supported in cast iron chairs on stone block sleepers, set at a gauge of four feet. Their scope was to be greatly increased in later years, as extensions were made.

Both tramways operated on the same principle. Loaded wagons carrying two or three tons were largely self-propelling down the moderate gradients under the control of a brakesman. Frequent pass-bys prevented the undue building up of traffic and after the coal had been discharged into canal boats, the wagons were hauled back to the pits by horses.

Eventually a system of horse dollies or dandy carts was introduced. These low trailers behind the coal wagons carried the horse and brakesman on the downhill journey, so the horse was then available for manoeuvring in the pass-bys.

During this period, as in the previous forty years, the bulk of the output was disposed of along the canal. Landsales continued at individual pits and particularly at the sub-depots of Walkden Moor and Dixon Green.

Coke production had been established by the Duke at Worsley yard, Walkden and Dixon Green and the Trust expanded this side of the business in the hope of meeting the demands for coke. Under the Trust these installations, still largely the 'bee hive' type, were modernised and new ovens added. By 1835 the output of coke from 24 ovens at Worsley was 225 tons per week. Walkden (12 ovens) produced 125 tons per week and Dixon Green (14 ovens) 135 tons per week.

In the hope of supplying the demand for locomotive fuel for the new railways, twelve extra ovens were added at Worsley in 1839. Others were planned but never built, as the contract of supply was not renewed.

Mine boats at Worsley

New management, laws and trade unions

The structure of the Trust as originally formed had numerous shortcomings; many of the years 1825-60 were spent ironing these out. Not only was control divorced from the beneficiary, but events unforeseen by the Duke radically altered the trading position of the Trustees. Chief of these events was the coming of the railways. Opposition by the Trust was intense: they were involved in about 170 Parliamentary battles against railways, the object being to protect their canal interests. Litigation did not come cheap and opposition to the Liverpool-Manchester railway alone cost the Trust £10,000. Eventually they relented in this case, even selling land for railway purposes in Salford. Really the Trustees were in a dilemma, for their beneficiary, Lord Stafford, was a major shareholder in the Liverpool to Manchester railway.

By the mid-1820s funds were at a low ebb, with the canals incurring heavy maintenance costs. Under the terms of the Trust, all profit had to be paid to the beneficiary, except a very small amount. The Duke had also left a capital amount to be used for maintenance, but both these sums proved to be inadequate, for under the railway threat improvements had to be made to remain competitive. Eventually Lord Stafford advanced £40,000 for improvements, as a life loan to the Trust to protect his income.

It is unlikely that much of this injection of cash found its way to the collieries, which contributed less than a third of all the profits in the overall balance sheet of the Trust at this time. The pits were in a rather neglected state. Fluctuations in the output were regular during the course of any one year and Bradshaw even tendered for driving tunnels on the Liverpool-Manchester railway to keep his colliers in employment.

The shaky structure of the Trust was being undermined by two opposing forces, its superintendent and its beneficiary. The superintendent, who had a concern for the Trust's future,

wished to present an Estate Bill to Parliament to break the restrictions on borrowing and investment under the terms of the Duke's will. Meanwhile, the Staffords squeezed the Trust for all they could get to finance their own interests. Their principal agent, James Loch, was a very capable man with diverse experience. His contacts with the Northumberland area gave him full realisation of the potential of railways. Also, as a first-rate businessman he viewed the workings of the Trustees with suspicion.

Events were brought to a head in 1833 by another financial crisis. The ageing Bradshaw was becoming more irascible and withdrawn, and to complicate matters further Stafford, by now the Duke of Sutherland, died. He left his own property to his eldest son and the Bridgewater interest passed to his second son, Francis; James Loch continued to act as agent to both.

For the Trust, the crunch came with the demand for the repayment to the Stafford Estate of

Lord Stafford's loan. This, together with poor balance sheets, made Bradshaw impossible to deal with and James Loch manoeuvred him into retiring in 1834. The new superintendent was James Sothern, Bradshaw's assistant and son of the Duke's late principal agent. He was appointed with the object of giving some control to the beneficiary who, under the Duke's wishes, had changed his name to Francis Egerton. However, Loch did not trust Sothern and openly wished to be rid of him.

Sothern had other ideas and intended being the boss, impounding the Trust deed to secure his position. Only after many lawsuits was he brought to terms, which included acting under the Egertons' directions on major items of policy. Eventually Sothern agreed to resign in March 1837 and James Loch was appointed superintendent, thus giving the ultimate control to Francis Egerton and allowing a consistent policy to be followed in the direction of the Trust's affairs.

James Loch was a man of wide responsibilities who had to rely on delegation. He continued to watch over the Sutherland estates both in Staffordshire and Scotland (where

A hurrier in a coal pit in 1841 - a Victorian engraving

he had supervised the Highland clearances), and was also agent to the Earl of Carlisle. On taking up the superintendent trustee's position, he became the M.P. for Brackley as well. With these posts, he had enough to do formulating policy and needed an experienced industrial agent. Through his contacts with the Earl of Dudley's estate, where he was auditor, Loch obtained the services of their agent's son. Backed with the promise of advice from his father, George Fereday Smith was duly appointed deputy superintendent in March 1837. He had an industrial background, had studied mining and geology and, after working as a surveyor, had helped engineer the Birmingham-Gloucester railway. He was only 25 when appointed by the Trustees.

Under the new management, a complete overhaul of the administrative structure took place, with central control from Worsley. Loch also pruned administration costs. Competitive tendering for most services was introduced instead of automatically using the Worsley yard staff, though it is likely that this move applied more to the canal works than to the colliery needs. Of direct concern to the

collieries was the fact that both Loch and Francis Egerton often considered selling the pits or, as they grew more dilapidated, leasing the working of them.

The lack of investment under the terms of the Trust had made it difficult for the pits to produce coal efficiently, a situation which was partially righted in the years 1837-39 by a heavy outlay on the collieries and the by-products plants. This sufficed until the trade slump of 1842, but then costs were savagely cut and many colliers were discharged, the pits being allowed to fall back into their neglected state until about 1846.

Until the late 1840s, most development in the pits had been paid for by Francis Egerton, who had other financial commitments. To ease this stranglehold on the Trust, an Estate Bill was submitted to Parliament in 1851. The Act sanctioned more liberal powers of raising capital, £150,000, in fact, being borrowed forthwith. The Act also eased restrictions on the sale or lease of Trust land for private building, much needed in the Walkden and Roe Green areas for housing and other industry.

James Loch died in June 1855 and was succeeded by Algernon

Lord Francis Egerton, later First Earl of Ellesmere

Egerton, the third son of Francis Egerton. Virtually without experience of industrial administration, Algernon Egerton accepted office on condition he would resign if required. His avowed plans were to raise more coal and sink more pits. This appointment gave complete control of the Trust to the beneficiary, though the benefits of the new superintendent were felt mainly by Fereday Smith, now the general manager. These two men made good partners, major reconstructions commenced and

The New Hall, Worsley, 1847

funds were freed for other developments to the collieries. This use of capital loans proved to be better than borrowing directly from the family.

Throughout the period up to 1870 the administrative centre was the Old Hall at Worsley, with subsidiary offices at Castlefield, Manchester, and at Runcorn for the canal interests. The Duke's Red Brick Hall had been left as the residence for the superintendent trustee. When the Egerton family took up residence at Worsley in 1837 they used part of the Old Hall; later, after the removal from office of Sothern, they moved to the Red Brick Hall. Plans were made for a new mansion for them, which was to be a Gothic edifice to the south of Leigh Road, and work on this and its landscaped gardens had been completed in 1846, when the Red Brick Hall was demolished. In the same year, Francis Egerton had been created the first Earl Ellesmere. Wishing to extend his landed interests, the Earl purchased the estates in Boothstown and Tyldesley previously owned by Bradshaw. These were separately administered from the Trust estates, but the coal was leased to the Trust.

Of the many facets of the Trustees' business interests, their incursion into the Wigan coalfield is possibly the least documented. The Wigan outpost of the collieries centred on Orrell and Pemberton, where the Duke first leased coal in 1790. Leases were still being contracted there by the Trustees in the 1840s and in all, 14 parcels of land were leased, most of them from the Blundell family. Apart from the value of the coal raised, the Pemberton collieries gave strategic value to the diversities of the Trust. They certainly had membership of trade associations in the Wigan area, keeping their transport and coal interests protected.

The mid-nineteenth century saw the beginning of the influence of legislation affecting the regulation of coal mines. Safe working practice had hitherto been left to the owner's conscience and the good sense of the colliers. The results usually left much to be desired. The 1842 report previously mentioned did not indicate a high level of safety consciousness at the Trustees' pits. The prime causes were most likely the reluctance of the men to be employed on dead, or non-productive work, and the lack of capital for safer working equipment. It was perhaps fortunate that the availability of funds for safe working coincided with the periods of compulsory inspection of collieries.

A series of Mines Regulation Acts placed the safe working of the pits high on the manager's list of priorities. From the introduction of the 1850 Act, which made inspection compulsory, regular visits by the district inspector, Mr Dickinson, are noted in the Trust's records. From these it is seen that the Trust and their colliery staff made every effort to maintain as safe an environment as possible in those days of hand labour.

The rules of the regulating Acts were implemented, often against the prejudice of the men. Summonses for smoking in the pit were issued until the practice had been stamped out. A series of rules for 'The Conduct of Work in the Collieries' was introduced by the Trust in 1856. These separated into general and special rules to meet specific incidents and the colliery agent, Mr Ridyard, kept a signed receipt from each manager and underlooker issued with a copy.

Mr Fereday Smith also exercised firm control on his manager, in introducing a system of daily reports on the state of the colliery ventilation, roof control and the winding gear. In these the colliery manager, Thomas Wallwork, also had to account for his movements, stating which pits had been visited. In these very illuminating reports, notes of deaths are surprisingly infrequent, the usual causes being roof falls, falling down ladder pits and gas explosions. The attitude of the colliery manager is best revealed by a comment in his own report in the 1860s: 'There is concern for safe working here, which is in the best interest of the Trust.'

During the lifetime of the Duke,

WORSLEY, July 30th, 1842.

The evils which an over crowded population entails upon the poorer classes of society make it necessary to consider in what manner this may, with the most ease, and with the least interference with their comforts, be diminished gradually, and finally removed altogether. There can be no doubt that early and ill considered marriages between very young persons is one great cause of these evils. Marriages contracted without forethought, and without any consideration as to the means of future support and maintenance of children.

Such marriages should be discouraged for the sake of the individuals themselves as well as for that of their parents and neighbours.

Such marriages receive great encouragement upon the Bridgewater Estate, from the parties being permitted to reside in their parents' dwellings after marriage, thereby producing other serious evils and inconvenience.

It is therefore hereby intimated, that after the 1st day of October next, no cottage tenant shall permit any newly married son or daughter to take up their residence in their house, without leave in writing from Mr. Fereday Smith, or Mr. Robt. Lansdale, as the case may be, or the tenant himself will be put under notice.

Mr. Lansdale will fill up any cottage now vacant from those cottages which contain more than one family, taking great care that the vacancy thus made shall not be filled up by an extra family or lodger.

JAMES LOCH.

Resolving a housing and a moral crisis

workers were largely glad to come to Worsley and the twin advantages of a paternalistic atmosphere and an expanding economy aided recruitment. In the period of the first two superintendents, the changed economic situation caused a reduction in the standards of living conditions, which came to be described as 'The lowest state of ignorance and degradation' in a social report of 1846.

When Francis Egerton took control, he set about many much-needed social reforms. Both he and his wife Harriet had a deep sense of duty to their employees, and provided the means for moral and physical improvement in the belief that this would lead to a better class of worker. Their residence in Worsley was in itself an attempt to atone for the years of absenteeism and jointly they succeeded in creating a local bountiful and paternal estate.

Their many benefactions included churches and schools at Worsley and Walkden, reading rooms and a medical dispensary; they also attempted to control the drunkenness and immorality that had plagued the district. Their agent, James Loch, became the iron hand behind the benevolence; it was he who distributed numerous handbills among the estate tenants warning them of the consequences of immoral behaviour, eviction being the ultimate deterrent. Not surprisingly, most tenants were anxious to remain. Houses were generally of the four-room type, with a small yard, and the estate charged a rent of £3 a year for those cottages newly built.

All improvements benefited the estate as a whole. Of more direct interest to the colliers were the efforts made to remove women and children from the pits. Proposals for alternative employment for women by introducing cotton factories to the estate had been discussed by the Trust in 1838 and after direct pressure from Lady Ellesmere instructions were given in July 1841 not to employ any more girls in the pits.

Legislation was imminent on this subject. In discussions with Lord Ashley, the force behind the

proposed Bill, the Trust and particularly Loch argued against its immediate effect but it is likely that this viewpoint was based on fear of unemployment for those removed from the pits rather than on any disagreement with the purpose of the Bill. On the passing of the 1842 Act, prohibiting the employment of women, girls and boys aged under ten in the pits, the Trust implemented it fully. In fact they tried to make the age limit twelve for boys, but were pressurised by the men into retaining the age of ten in some pits.

Steps were also taken to overcome the problem of the redundant girls and women. The older ones were found work at farms on the estate, while younger girls could be sent to Lady Ellesmere's Domestic Training School. This foundation, added to the Walkden School, gave a year's residential training in domestic skills and positions in service were found for the girls completing the course. As an incentive, parents received 5p per week to compensate for loss of wages.

During the period of management by the first two superintendents, the colliers had become among the

lowest paid in the South Lancashire Coalfield. At Worsley, a sliding scale of wages had been established, based on the selling price of coal, which gave an average wage of under 50p per week in the Trustees' pits against almost 75p at other local pits. Colliers were also paid monthly, putting a great strain on the family budgets of the more improvident.

The worst of the colliers' grievances were attended to by the Egertons' managers. From January 1843 wages began to be paid every fortnight, as was usual at other local pits. In addition, pay offices were established at several parts of the estate to prevent colliers from being tempted to spend a large proportion of their wages on drink.

As actual pay rates per ton were comparable with those of other employers, inefficient overmanning had to be tackled and numbers of superfluous colliers were discharged, with Mr Ridyard making the selection. The long established system of advancement up the pay scale according to age had to be severely restricted, the approval of Mr Smith or Mr Ridyard being needed before a junior could become a coal getter or hewer. These measures, whilst

Colliers, 1842

regretted by the management, increased the efficiency of the concern and eventually led to higher wages.

Having put to rights many of their inherited social evils, the Egertons and their managers made some provisions for their older workers. In the late 1840s a pension scheme for long service employees was started. Completely non-contributory, it assured a reasonable standard of life in old age, with the usual rate of benefit for manual workers set at 25p per week or about one third of the average wage. Salaried employees did rather better, depending on their status and length of service.

Another benefaction of direct advantage to the Trust as employers came with the introduction of evening classes for the colliers. During the mid-1850s, Mr W Traice was engaged as 'Lecturer in practical science to the Colliers' and was paid as such by the Trustees. Classes were held at the Walkden Schools covering most of the technical aspects of coal mining, and these raised levels of skill in the workforce. He also held more recreational classes, which eventually had a wide following. Mr Traice was still being employed by the Trust in the 1870s.

It would appear that the Egertons' efforts to produce a better standard of living for all on the estate had largely succeeded.

An expanding sub-structure of welfare provisions and self-sufficiency by the tenants themselves made many of the earlier welfare foundations obsolete. The medical dispensary, for example, had outlived its usefulness by 1870. Correspondence between James Ridyard and the Dowager Countess Ellesmere, as managers, concluded that as subscriptions in Walkden were only £6.40 that year from a dwindling circle, benefits were to be paid until Christmas 1871 and then the scheme was to be wound up.

Trades unions had a rather slow growth in the Worsley district. Under the Duke's paternal care, organised labour movements had been largely irrelevant and the goodwill generated in the previous century inbred to provide an almost feudal loyalty in the time of the first two superintendents and absentee landlords. True, several Trust employees were convicted of trades oath taking in 1812, food riots had occurred in that year and sentences of transportation had been placed on Worsley men. But the Egertons soon established themselves as worthy local leaders and started their many benefactions, and the district maintained its tradition of being an estate, with due deference being given to its head. Full acceptance of their obligations by the Egertons helped maintain good relations for a long time in the majority of cases.

With the easing of the laws on the formation of trades unions, individual colliery districts formed purely locally effective lodges, and by 1840 the main aim was to have a national structure. Owing to influences outside the estate, in the Wigan collieries particularly, and to the more rapid communications available, organised labour had started to assert itself in Worsley. A wage strike in 1841 collapsed because of the duplicity of James Loch. The majority were given words of advice in a handbill; the more militant were dismissed and evicted. Chartism and the ensuing plug riots of 1842 largely passed Worsley by. Not only did the colliers stay at work, except when the Trust closed the pits for fear of an attack from outside the district, but several parties were paid 'To be on duty at the pits on Walkden Moor during the disturbances.' An address of loyalty was also presented to Lord Egerton, presumably matching the mood of the majority. However, such deferences were to cease within the next few years.

Outside influences, particularly the nationally based Miners' Association, which had described Worsley as 'a stronghold of corruption' and noted that the pay there was only 'a few pence more than poor law relief,' now began to attract active union membership. A branch of the Miners' Association was formed with several lodges to serve the district, gaining about two thirds of the Trustees' colliers as members, and strikes were fomented in 1843, 1846 and 1851. However, the national structure eventually collapsed owing to employer pressure, leaving the local lodges to form the Worsley Miners' Association, a movement which had a rather nebulous existence during the middle years of the nineteenth century.

A miners' strike procession at Walkden Monument, 1882

Steam power and the decline of the Navigable Level

In the period 1840-70 changes in policy, investment and output had as big an effect on the concern as the Duke's innovations had in the previous century. Whilst many factors, including the canal and Navigable Level, had made the collieries viable in previous years, a more aggressive outlook now evolved. The inability to compete in a free market had to be overcome by major redevelopment and new investment in shaft sinkings. Less radically, there had to be a management structure capable of directing efficiently the extraction of the coal, using up to date mining technology.

As mentioned earlier, output doubled in the 1830s. By contrast, the 1840s was a period of stagnation, with production declining. A national slump had partially been responsible, particularly in 1848, and trade continued at a low ebb until 1850, when apparently selling prices were so low that royalties were barely met. In these years the overall capacity of the Trustees' collieries had increased, so whilst the figures below may seem to indicate a rise in output, spread over the increased number of pits this was not the case. By 1858, however, full recovery had begun and production markedly increased for some years thereafter.

Coal output 1830-1870:

1830	165,000 tons
1840	283,700 tons
1848	254,000 tons
1850	278,700 tons
1860	371,400 tons
1870	550,000 tons

There were many factors contributing to this trend, primarily the more settled nature of the Trust's management, with its avowed intention of raising output. A settled and still growing Lancashire industrial economy provided the outlet for the increased effort. Closer to the heart of the matter, the many capital investments and social provisions of the Trust and the Egertons laid the basis for a relatively trouble-free coalfield.

On the debit side, the long feared threat of railway-borne coal competition for the Manchester market materialised in the 1850s, when several lines could supply the city. To counteract this, a diversity of outlets was established and the general upsurge of demand absorbed the increased output. Larger quantities of coking coal were required by the local gas supply industries and the Trust supplied most local towns with cannel coal, an ideal base for the gas making process. There was also a growing demand for coke, which the Trust attempted to meet by increasing production.

At the collieries themselves, the main change in operations in mid-century was the increased depth of coal getting. There had been a general exhaustion of shallower reserves, as indicated by the abandonment of the Upper Navigable Level. Similarly, most of the branches of the Main Level had been worked out, as had the Chaddock section at Boothstown, so the Trust was forced to abandon the economically sensible policy of working the shallower reserves. (Hitherto most workings had been far less than 150 yards deep.) By the late 1850s there was an overall progression to what may be termed medium depth pits - in the 100 to 300 yards range. This diversification of working area and depth also meant the almost complete adoption of steam powered shaft services.

In many cases the older pits based on the Navigable Level were given a new lease of life by deepening. New sinkings alongside the Level also tapped the reserves further down. The advantage of this policy was the still-economic transport system, in the form of a trunk haulage route direct to the canal, where most of the Trust's output was distributed. Capital investment had to be poured in to develop these lower reserves, but the loosening of financial restrictions outlined earlier helped. It is reported that some £23,000 per year had to be spent on capital plant and sinkings for the collieries throughout the sixties.

As may be expected in a concern covering such an area and a multitude of pits, development in any period had many aspects. Pits can be considered to be developing as they are worked along the coal seam in the normal course of events. Other sections may be developed by tapping a new seam or having new machinery installed to speed the process. Completely new sinkings were yet another

Edgefold Colliery alongside Walkden Road, photographed in 1952

form of development at the collieries within this period.

By the start of the 1840s, production had been concentrated on four main districts. In Deane and Farnworth, where the cannel coal was still in great demand, workings based on the Navigable Level continued in operation, as they did in the Plodder and Dean Moor seams. Several pits also worked these three seams, including Lords Moss, Howarth's Field, Watergate pit, Sapling, Culberts, Fray's, Eckersley's and Fletcher's Field pits.

Further south along the line of the Navigable Level, seams with water transport were worked at Burton's Garden, Barracks pit, the reconstructed Magnall's pit and Edgefold. On the two flanks, the pits had to make do with landsales or cartage to the new tramways, which at this time served only a few collieries directly. To the east, Sanderson's pits had been fully opened up and were producing well. The group of sinkings made at Wardley in the late 1830s was producing coal, with the last pit in the group at Lansdale's Field being ready for the new decade. The west flank had as productive units the Tynesbank pits on Hilton Lane, as well as Burgess Land pits; this group also included the Mather's Fold pit as a newly completed shaft.

Of the many types of development at existing collieries, only the most

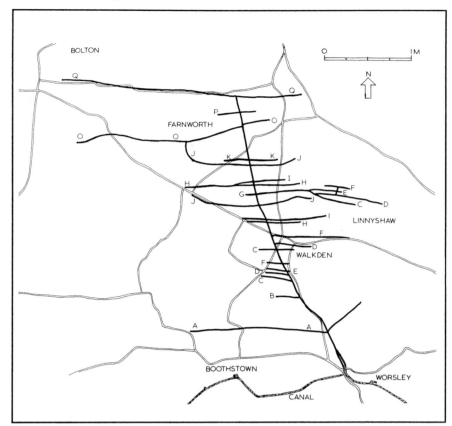

Main navigable levels (See seam sequence chart, page 2)

noteworthy can be mentioned here. Most of the pits with any prospective life had their winding gear improved in this period and the method of transporting coal underground also changed radically from the 1840s. These general improvements will be outlined later.

Whilst deeper navigable levels had been introduced before the turn of the century, it was these middle

years that saw their multiplication and extension. At first, they may have been as an interim measure with the exhaustion of shallower reserves along the Navigable Level corridor. Later, deepening the existing pits became the easy solution, as the new levels could be used to carry the coal. Most of these new or extended deeper levels served to connect with pits that were sunk in the 1840s, so as well as being productive in their own right, they were speedily driven to give the new pits the benefit of water transport.

Of these levels, the most extensive were those driven in the Croumbouke and Seven Feet seams to join Edgefold low levels with City and Gatley pits. These shafts, just inside the Tyldesley boundary near Mosley Common, required navigable levels over a mile long to reach them and the tunnels proved to be a well used route providing transport, assistance with ventilation and drainage. A further connection from the reconstructed Magnall's pits near Walkden ran to meet the new sinkings at Madams Wood at Peel. Whilst not navigable all the way to Peel, this level in the Seven Feet seam did make connections in the workings.

Magnall's Colliery alongside Wilfred Road, Walkden. The Royal British Legion Club was built on the site

Pits on the Walkden Moor section of the Level were included in this development. Burton's Garden pit near Walkden centre had worked the Black seam from 1820 about 40 yards below the Main Level. An axial level was then cut to the neighbouring White seam and extensive working took place in both seams on each flank for some 800 yards. At the termination of the east level, a further tunnel headed south to meet the Brassey seam, with workings some 700 yards long. A shaft to the deeper Seven Feet seam worked a similar area.

The most noteworthy deepening of a shaft at the northern end of the Navigable Level was at Tonge's Field near Dixon Green. This sinking in 1841 reached the Dean Moor seam 55 yards below the Main Level and extensive working took place on both flanks. Most of this work had been carried out during the 1840s in what amounted to a coal trade slump, so the investment here was no more than was needed to maintain productive capacity.

However, the new shafts and complete collieries opened out in the 1850s and 1860s changed the whole nature of the Trustees' operations. Deeper than previous workings and with equipment equal to any other coalfield, the many pits sunk in the middle years of the century maintained the profitability of the Trust, and of their subsequent owners.

Whilst Sanderson's pit near Roe Green worked deeper coal than other shafts in the districts, the first major new sinking started in 1843. This site at Coppice Field near Wardley Hall was to become a substantial colliery, sending much of its output down the Wardley tramway. Initially there were two shafts 200 yards deep for winding and pumping, then a further upcast shaft with a ventilation furnace was added. Most of the ironwork for the site, including the chimney cap, came from the estate of the Earl of Dudley, with whom the Trust had many connections.

Production at Coppice Field started in 1845, working the Binn, Croumbouke, Brassey and Seven Feet seams. In later years, many

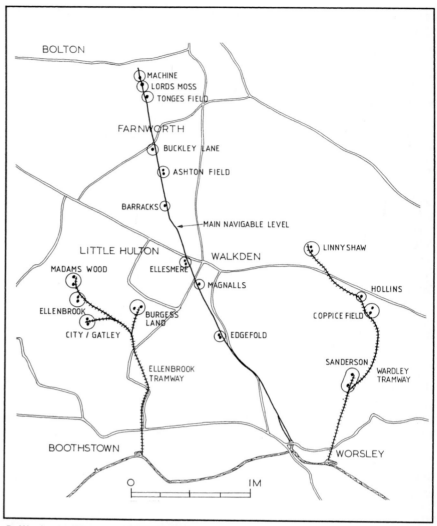

Collieries and transport 1860-1870

surface buildings were erected there, when elementary coal preparation by screening started.

Perhaps to keep a balance between the flanks of the coalfield, the Trust transferred their sinkers to Madams Wood, Little Hulton, where work started in 1847. A year later, two shafts sunk 110 yards to the Croumbouke, Brassey and Seven Feet seams were producing coal. The usual shaft services were provided and a tramway extension laid for coal distribution to the canal at Boothstown. The twin pits of City and Gatley in New Manchester, together with those at Burgess Land, completed the group of pits served by this western tramway. City pit had been developed about 1840 with Gatley a little later. Many interconnections in the workings were made between these pits working the same seams, and the navigable connections mentioned previously aided many of the ancillary services, although these were provided at each pit.

The sinking crews saw out the decade by working at the Delph in Over Hulton and forming Number 2 pit at Sanderson's, Roe Green, the object in both cases being to provide auxiliary shafts to existing pits. Delph pit, sunk to the Plodder seam in 1848, wound coal for the Bolton market. There were plans for a tramway between Delph and Watergate pit to the south, but there is no record of it having been made. Watergate pit had been reconstructed from Level access shafts to become a self-contained pit working the Cannel and Dean Moor seams. Winding and pumping facilities were installed and a furnace was built to ventilate the pit in 1859.

These initial provisions of pits capable of a sustained output were ready to meet the upsurge in demand in the 1850s. The collieries' efforts appear to have been largely taken up with production in the first years of the decade; few new sinkings were started, but several shafts were deepened and improved, though this work is traceable only in slight references in officials' notes. The next major phase of shaft sinking started once the new Trust management had settled in and formed a team of officials capable of directing operations on a grander scale than previously in Worsley. Much coal still lay beneath the Navigable Level workings, and many of the relatively new pits were sited too near the outcrop to have a long life expectancy at the increased rate of output. What quantities of coal the shafts could handle had also been seriously considered, as a larger diameter shaft can accommodate bigger cages of tubs. Until this time, most shafts had been 8 to 10 feet in diameter, but all the shafts in the next phase were made at least 12 feet in diameter.

The first of the new pits to work the deep coal beneath the Navigable Level was sited at Ashton's Field near the old inclined plane. Work started in 1853 sinking two shafts, which were deepened several times in the next ten years. The colliery worked the Doe, Five Quarters, Trencherbone, Plodder and Dean Moor seams, eventually reaching a depth of 500 yards. In parallel with this work, the old Navigable Level access shaft at Buckley Lane was deepened in 1862 to meet and work the same seams and act as a ventilation shaft to Ashton's Field, a furnace being installed at Buckley Lane for the purpose.

The other major sinkings to be made alongside the Navigable Level were started in 1865. Two shafts that were to form the Ellesmere Colliery were sunk at Walkden next to the main road to Manchester, superseding the old shafts of Causewayside pits, which were abandoned. The new shafts reached 300 yards to the Doe, Five Quarters and Trencherbone seams and connection was made to the Level, as at Ashton's Field, for coal transport and pump discharge. In 1867 an air pit was started further north alongside the Level, with the working and ventilation shafts being linked in 1870. The same year, coal from the new site was boated down the Level for the first time.

The first colliery designed from the outset to have very deep shafts

was that at Berryfield in Linnyshaw, known officially as Linnyshaw pit. The shafts to the Binn, Croumbouke, Brassey and Seven Feet seams were over 300 yards deep and 12 feet in diameter. Furnace ventilation was provided, as were iron guide rods for the shaft cages. All preparations had been made to deal with a large output, including a tramway connection when the colliery started production in 1860. Progress was rapid in the workings despite a serious explosion in 1864, when it took several days to persuade the colliers it was safe to return to work. Haulage jig brows of up to 400 yards long came into use at this pit, although they often proved more troublesome than the shorter ones. However, Linnyshaw had been a trouble free pit to sink, and its working area seems also to have been free of the many small geological problems that beset the collieries on the western flank of the Worsley coalfield.

With Linnyshaw in production, the professional sinkings crew the

Trustees had assembled under their foreman Daniel Timmins moved to the west. Initially called Stonehouse Pits, the 500-yard deep shafts of Mosley Common Colliery proved to be the most difficult the Trustees ever sank. Work started on the two main shafts in 1862, and soon that year excessive water was met with. Eventually massive pumps had to be installed, using 80 tons of coal per week to power them, and water winding had to be utilised regularly in order to assist the pumps. These setbacks threw the whole programme out of schedule. Permanent pit head buildings could not be erected until 1866, when work started in the Croumbouke seam with the making of wagon roads. Extensive lodge rooms were also made at the pit bottom to store the water for 'off peak' pumping. In 1867 connection was made with the air pit, Number 3 shaft, and it was not until 1869 that full arrangements for cage winding had been completed. There appear to have been many temporary provisions, owing to the delays. Even the ventilation furnace was described

The level at Ashton's Field Pit

in 1869 as 'a small one, until we can get a better one'. Discussions about the quantity of coal that it would be possible to wind were still being held in 1870.

The delays caused by the problems at Mosley Common had repercussions throughout the western flank of the Trust's coalfield. Many of the existing collieries were coming to the end of their useful lives, and the intention was to transfer the workforces to Mosley Common. As early as 1862, Madams Wood Colliery had an inrush of water from old outcrop workings in the Croumbouke seam. So much mud was swept into the workings that even primitive chain and rag pumps proved ineffective. It was optimistically noted in 1868 that 'all the coal will soon be worked out at Madams Wood pits, but not until we are ready to transfer the men to Mosley Common.'

Unfortunately, little progress had been made by the end of 1869, when Mr Wallwork again reported, 'The coal at Madams Wood is worked out, coal at Gatley Brassey seam worked through the crop and at Coppice Field we are worked to the barriers.'

Work was found for the colliers at all sorts of places in the old pits to keep the labour forces together, but this led to difficulties in supervision. The colliers were well distributed in the old workings, so the underlookers had more places and men to keep right than they could give proper attention to.

Whether planned as a means of overcoming the delays at Mosley Common or as a separate venture, another colliery was constructed in the district. This was the Ellenbrook pit, situated on land near Common Head, New Manchester, belonging to the

Trustees of the Dame Dorothy Leigh charity. The main shaft, started in 1864, reached the Croumbouke coal a year later, when work was started on Number 2 shaft, the upcast. The pit also worked the Brassey and Seven Feet seams at a depth of 210 yards. Full production had been reached by September 1867, and connection made to the tramway. Ellenbrook pits certainly seem to have been an interim measure as they closed in 1887, having had a much shorter life than usual for a Trustee pit of this period.

By the time most of the sinking problems had been overcome at Mosley Common, reserves were running low at the pits to the east in Roe Green and Wardley. Coppice Field was rapidly reaching its barriers between adjacent owners, whilst Sanderson's pits had serious geological problems. To extend the life of the pits,

Mosley Common Colliery before reconstruction, and typical of the investment at the larger Bridgewater Trustees pits

'downbrow mining' had been resorted to. The 1,000-yard long main dip tunnel had followed the dip of the seam until the angle of dip decreased almost to nothing. This led Mr Wallwork to report that 'in the last few years Sandersons has been plagued with soft and tender roofs which make it expensive to work, and some places hardly safe to work at all.' The numerous sinkings of the late 1830s in Wardley, the 'Field' pits, had proved expensive to sink and work, and without too much of a future. Clearly a fresh start was needed.

Following the lead of Mosley Common, a new, deep, modern colliery was sunk at Wardley near the Hall. This colliery was known as the Bridgewater pits during the time of the Trust and in later years as Sandhole. As with Mosley Common, a three-shaft configuration was decided upon and work started in 1865 on the first shaft, where progress was steady and uneventful. In August 1867 the second working shaft was begun, along with a connection to the intended air pit. For this shaft they used one of the sinkings of the later 1830s at Hollins Field in Wardley; it had been deepened previously, so little extra work was needed to prepare the shaft for its new role. Yet it was not until 1871 that a furnace was installed at this air pit, and coal production got under way. Initially the Black and Doe seams were worked at a depth of 400 yards, although the shafts were subsequently deepened to the Cannel seam at 550 yards. To ventilate this seam, the air pit needed to be 460 yards deep.

All this work put the Trustees in a very advantageous position with regard to the productive capacity of their new pits. Nearly all the capacity from the mid-century onwards came from under their own land or where existing leases were held. This avoided the expense of leasing further land. The lease details between the Trust and Lord Ellesmere's Estate are intricate, but royalties were certainly paid regularly, and it is doubtful if any favours were shown in lease terms.

As important as the new pits to the successful working of the collieries were the changes made to the staff

structure. Changes in the Trust altered the accounting procedures, but the nature of staff duties was also affected by the wider spread of effort, technical requirements and output. Taking an overall view of the collieries at the start of the 1840s, some 30 active pits and branch navigable levels spread over about 12 square miles of land had to be controlled. The simple line of command described earlier had become woefully inadequate, particularly where technical expertise was required. With the many ties that both the Trust and its employees had with Staffordshire, it isn't surprising that much staff recruiting went on there.

The most senior colliery posts of agent and viewer were held by people whose families had several generations of service behind them, but by the 1840s the incumbents were unfortunately too advanced in years for active colliery supervision. One of the earliest appointments of a Staffordshire man, who was subsequently of great value, was in 1819, when Thomas Wallwork began his employment as an underlooker.

In the early years of his service he was largely in charge of driving navigable levels, progressed to inspector in the collieries in 1860 and by 1864 to foreman inspector. By 1850 the old agent, John Pickup, had retired and John Ridyard, the viewer, had been promoted to colliery agent. A further coal sales agent or wharfinger, Thomas Kent, had been appointed in 1854 to superintend sales at Worsley basin. The Trust's deputy superintendent, later general manager, Fereday Smith, was also a Staffordshire man. As a capable technician he saw the weaknesses in the staff team, one of the greatest of which was the lack of competent engineers familiar with the methods and machinery needed in deep mining. The Wardley sinkings, started as Fereday Smith took up his duties in 1837, confirmed this view. A Staffordshire engineer, Daniel Timmins, was engaged in 1841 to supervise machinery and sinkings and it was he who oversaw most of the initial development of the 1840s. With the many proposed sinkings of the 1850s imminent, another Staffordshire man, Edward Bagot, entered the Trust's service as shaft sinker in 1846. Solely and

Linnyshaw Colliery, Wardley

continuously employed on this task, he supervised all the sinking work done by the Trust until his retirement in 1878.

Yet another technical function previously done rather haphazardly by the viewer and his assistant was the recording of where work was taking place. This was a second failing of the Worsley collieries noticed by Fereday Smith. It is important to record where coal is being worked, both from a safety aspect and to ensure that royalty boundaries are kept. The various Mines Regulations Acts also made the keeping of accurate plans obligatory. By 1850 a dialler, or underground surveyor, with a draughtsman as assistant, was employed to keep the plans of the workings up to date.

With the wider spread of independent pits by the end of the 1850s, there were further changes in the surface and underground staffs. In 1856 Daniel Timmins retired as engineer and was replaced by his son Jesse, with Daniel continuing as assistant agent until 1863. Thomas Wallwork became foreman inspector over all the collieries in 1864, with eight underlookers distributed throughout the concern, to resolve the day-to-day problems and supervise the men. The number of underlookers grew as the new deep pits grew, and changes to personnel on retirement are noted in the salary payment books of the Trust.

It is evident from surviving reports that Mr Wallwork had wide ranging interests and powers within the collieries. Whilst nominally in charge of the pitmen, he was also concerned with surface details. The many entries in his reports break down into a few general categories which may be summarised as: maintaining output and safety by enforcing the management's rules for conduct of work in the collieries; supervising the regular fortnightly measuring of the colliers' work, and surveying. This involved accompanying the check surveyors for the various coal lessees and, with Mr Ridyard, resolving differences in value in those workings where the coal was of poor quality. The men and

underlookers had to be advised on setting out new roadways or where geological problems were met with. Further responsibilities included helping to determine the actual site of new sinkings and making regular visits to check progress. His reports indicate that all the other staff were equally busy about their own tasks. The salary ledger records Mr Ridyard's duties as 'To attend to the returns necessary under the Mines inspection act, to take charge of the royalties account, to assist at the collieries proper, and assist the management in consideration of mining questions'. For these responsibilities Mr Ridyard and Thomas Wallwork received salaries of £250 and £180 respectively in 1864.

An important function of the staff was what has come to be termed labour relations. Individual and collective bargains were negotiated regularly, the usual system being to pay coal getting per ton or per yard advance at a set rate. The rates in 1842 were 12p per ton in pits, whilst cannel coal paid 11p and the less expensive Croumbouke coal in Walkden was graded as 7.5p per ton when riddled by the collier, 5.5p unriddled. Drivages in stone, termed metal work, or where small

faults had to be crossed, were open to negotiation. There was regular dissatisfaction with prices paid, leaving Mr Wallwork to drive a bargain.

By this time the Trust paid wages fortnightly, after work ceased on the Saturday, and the event was followed by play-Monday, when an unofficial holiday was taken. The management appear to have condoned this, as few records of disciplinary action exist. True holidays for the colliers included Christmas Day, New Year, Easter and Whit. Only a skeleton staff, to keep the furnaces and pumps going, worked Christmas Day; all the other days were used for making major repairs to the plant. Even play-Mondays were found convenient for this purpose.

By the 1860s, active trades unionism had taken hold in Worsley, involving the workforce in other than purely domestic disputes. Whilst none of these events proved disastrous to the Worsley coalfield, they show the trend away from a community totally loyal to a local patriarch. Some of the most noteworthy events were:

October 1863: Reductions in prices paid caused disputes and

The Bridgewater Trustees' offices, Bridgewater Road. The clock struck thirteen at one o'clock

stoppages in sympathy strikes. Meetings with colliers in Kearsley. Little Hulton colliers from Lord Kenyon's pits tried to get the Worsley men out.

Mid-1864: The men applied the sanction of stopping work at noon on Saturdays.

August 1865: Many Worsley men attended the great colliers' meeting at Hollingworth Lake. The repercussions lasted some days.

October 1865: In support of demands for better conditions of employment, the colliers reduced their daily output from ten to eight wagons.

September 1866: There were several instances of the men refusing to work with non-trades unionists. On 2nd September all the colliers were out and having a great demonstration march in the district.

February 1870: A major stoppage over pay which lasted some weeks.

Perhaps Mr Wallwork should have the last word about this dispute, for he records, 'The men are so full of wants I don't think they know what they do want.'

Methods of work in the Worsley

collieries in the mid-years of the nineteenth century also changed out of all recognition by previous standards. Many changes were as a result of working at a greater depth, others were introduced in line with the national trends in mining technology.

Equally important were those changes brought about or enforced by the many Mines Regulation Acts that came into force in these years. Whilst still a very labour intensive industry, coal mining was glad to increase productivity by any legitimate method, hence the introduction of such mechanical aids as could be proved to work in the arduous conditions underground. There were many instances of the Trust's colliery officials visiting other districts to observe new developments or different methods of working and full discussions were held to determine if the subject could be applied to local conditions.

The means of handling coal underground saw the most radical changes in mid-century. The passing of the 1842 Act, preventing women and children working underground as haulage hands, and Lady Ellesmere's efforts in the same direction forced the introduction of more enlightened methods. Obviously not even the

influence of Lady Ellesmere could change things overnight, but James Loch had set a deadline for the termination of this class of labour. The effect was such that in the workings based on the Navigable Level increased use had to be made of self-acting jig brows down to the branch levels. These inclines had to be fed from the individual stalls by older boys using wheeled tubs. Once this transition stage had been reached, further development in the workings led to the almost universal use of jig brows and pony haulage on rails to the loading points on the branch levels or pit bottoms.

Whilst by 1850 a very significant proportion of output came from pits unconnected with the navigable levels, these waterways still carried the bulk of production. Those branch levels still actively engaged in production, such as those in the Cannel and Dean Moor seams, were well maintained, as was the Main Level, and so heavy was the volume of traffic that absolute chaos followed a roof fall or the inadvertent sinking of a boat. Connections for the loading of coal from the new or deepened pits alongside the Level had to be arranged. Here the tubs came out of the cages into tipplers over a boat, or modifications had to be made to allow the continued use of the teeming holes or rock loading chutes in the sides of the levels. Complicated arrangements had to be made at both Edgefold and Ellesmere pits to avoid mixing the various grades of coal produced in the several seams worked.

Of the deeper navigable levels, the one at Magnall's pit on the Seven Feet seam appears to have been the most troublesome. As it was a deep level, constant pumping had to be employed, but unfortunately the pump proved to be far under-rated for its duty. The very wet winter of 1866-67 caused complete flooding of the level and workings, a situation worsened by the Engineer's neglect of the pump machinery. As each pit supplied its own coal for use in boilers, coal had to be imported along the Main Level to keep the pumps going at all. After a week of inaccessibility and after the floods had been pumped out, the work of clearing silt and sunken boats had to start. It was quite normal in very wet

Ellesmere Pit, Walkden, about 1900

weather to work these deeper levels with absolute minimum headroom to pass boats.

The rise in production during the 1850s and onwards meant an increase in the use of the Navigable Level even though it carried a decreasing proportion of the output. The Level's main drawback was the constant problem of capacity; the paradox of the Level being choked with boats, and yet not enough boats being available to carry the potential output, had gone on too long. By the late 1860s the Level carried a smaller proportion of output as other methods of transport extended to cover a wider area, though the levels did retain their popularity as a showpiece for visitors: the usual tour for VIPs, often friends of the Ellesmeres, included a visit to the workings at Edgefold pit.

Underground haulage at the newer pits settled into the use of wheeled tubs on rails with ponies pulling them. By the mid-1860s experiments were made with other types of haulage involving mechanical power. The down brow mine at Sanderson's had an engine-powered ropeway by 1866; whether this was driven by steam or compressed air is not known. Another type gradually introduced, and eventually widely used until late into the century,

involved rope haulage driven by rope gearing which passed up the shaft to an engine on the surface. Of particular interest on these rope haulages and jig brows is that Jesse Owen, the developer of the self-detaching winding hook, designed a similar device for use on haulages especially for the Trustees' pits.

The use of deeper shafts brought the consideration of winding gear to the fore. It is noticeable that in the 1850s and early 1860s the new sinkings had priority for equipment, therefore replacement of winding gear at the other active pits took place only gradually. In this transitional period ladder pits were still numerous for access to the Navigable Level-based workings; several water-balance engines likewise served at older pits. As obsolete plant came to be replaced, without interfering with production, problems sometimes arose on the sites. In 1868, for example, the new engine at Edgefold had been so positioned that the engine man could not see the top of the shaft and a signaller had to be employed to give directions.

The new equipment installed generally used wire ropes, iron shaft guides and double-deck cages, with relatively large horsepower, high pressure engines. The pair of Nasmyth

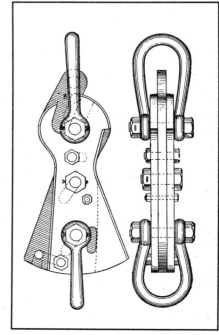

The Ormrod detaching-hook, in use at Bridgewater pits to prevent the overwinding of cages

vertical engines of 30" bore x 4'6" stroke, developing 175hp, installed at Ellesmere pits in 1866 were fairly typical of those used at this period.

With the increased emphasis on safety, wire ropes became common by the late 1860s; one of the last main pits to use hemp ropes was Edgefold, where it was noted in 1859 that 'The hemp rope had become badly frayed in use, it was well bound with twine and deemed safe to wind on'. Iron and steel wire ropes were costly to install and they were not immune to breakages, as the managers' reports show in several instances. Protection against overwinding came with the self-detaching hook; initially the Owen type had been installed by the Trust but by the 1880s the Ormrod hook had become the norm.

The actual hewing of coal had not altered in its physical requirements. Hand cutting still provided the output, although several small experiments with coal and rock cutting machines had been undertaken by the Walkden colliery yard staff in the late 1860s. But the primary changes in working methods had been in the layout of the work places. A Northumbrian style of pillar and stall working was tried in the late 1840s, which proved not entirely suitable to the seams of the

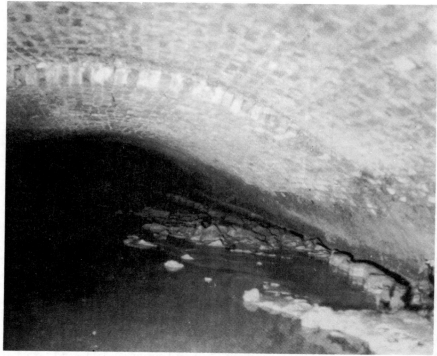

A sunken coal boat near the Ellesmere pit shaft

Worsley coalfield. Eventually, an optimum extraction cycle evolved, suitable for either Navigable Level or wagon way transport. From the Level, or roadway, rise brows were driven about 100 yards apart for a length of some 250 yards, obviously varying according to the seam gradient. Lifts of coal would then be removed on each side of these brows, starting at the top. These lifts or 'ribbings' were 14 yards wide on average. Props would then support the 'goaf edge' (the worked-out edge) and a ventilation course when subsequent lower lifts were worked. Through lack of supervision, these working places had reached up to 50 yards wide in places; although well propped, reprimands were issued as this width of working was declared unsafe.

Despite this management attitude to wide working spaces, visits were made to Staffordshire to examine their longwall working in 1866. By 1868 part of the Seven Feet seam was being worked on trial, 'all in one face, in the shape of long work'. The conservative colliers resented the system, although according to the manager it was demonstrably safe. Similar trials at Buckley Lane pits had two longwall faces in operation, though these experiments were conducted on the more solid coal of the centre of the coalfield. The

deeper pits to the west in the Ellenbrook district had a more broken structure with many small steps or faults in the geological strata.

Hand cutting of coal remained the most hazardous task in the pits and piecework rates caused the colliers to be their own worst enemies in this respect. The commonest cause of roof falls was the failure to set 'sprags' when undercutting the coal. Underlookers were specifically instructed to ensure sufficient props had been set by the colliers under their charge, to avoid falls and the costs in clearing them. Timber props and roof bars were the usual support in working places and most roadways, but these essential passages received special protection by a sheathing of brickwork at important junctions or when crossing faults, or poor strata. All shaft mouthings and pit bottom marshalling positions had their brick and mortar lining. Economy with materials is evidenced by the use of old boat sides for underground timbering. Cast iron tubbing to line shafts had been introduced at Lords Moss pit in 1868 but this method never replaced the usual practice of brick lining.

Ventilation of the workings received the due consideration of the technical staff. Regular

outbursts of black and fire-damp occurred and strenuous efforts were needed to clear properly the gas pockets. Correct coursing of the air through the workings became a more exact science, with the staff directing the placing of air doors and brattice cloths to control flows, but constant efforts were needed to keep air passages clear, as unproductive work was resented by the men. Up to the end of the 1870s furnaces were the usual method of producing currents of air in the Worsley pits and with the increased technical knowledge available, these could be made more efficient; full appreciation of the effects of outside air pressure and temperature allowed these factors to be taken into account too. Anemometers were bought for use in the pits to verify air flows, which by most reports were negligible in hot weather.

The furnaces themselves sometimes gave trouble. Fires in the strata above the furnace crown did happen and caused the pit to be closed whilst they were extinguished. Reciprocating air pumps and tin pipes to distribute air to the workings had been tried at Coppice Field in 1864, but there is no report on their effects. Steam jets in a shaft instead of a furnace were also tried, with no permanent installation being made.

Candles provided the usual

Looking across the west end of Blackleach Reservoir towards Blackleach Row, built in 1818

working light until well into the 1870s; the tendency was to use safety lamps only when testing for gas before starting a shift, or in places where known concentrations of fire-damp existed. Such a situation occurred on the deepening of Buckley Lane pit in 1862, when conditions were such that only locked safety lamps were deemed suitable. In later years the use of snuffing wires, poked through the gauze of the lamp to trim the wick whilst it was alight, had to be prohibited. Despite such precautions in known hazardous areas, regular explosions were caused by candle flames, particularly by boatmen's lights in the Navigable Level. Often the safety lamps were kept underground at the pit, and the lamproom itself at Burgess Land pit caused a fire in 1866.

As the area of operations and the number of individual pits increased, the need for buildings of all kinds at the pit banks also increased. Before 1850 only the engine house and perhaps a few sheds were required. With the increase in engine power and hence the number of boilers, the buildings grew in size. The relatively squat, square-section chimneys gave way to the round giants more often associated with factories. Boilers were set in multiple ranges alongside the brick-built engine houses with their usual round-headed windows. Noticeable differences occurred between the types of headstocks employed. Most of the reconstructed Navigable Level pits had goalpost structures of timber baulks with little or no back bracing, whereas lattice girder types with a pronounced brace were erected at the new deep sinkings such as Mosley Common and Bridgewater.

Each of these larger collieries operated on a more self-contained basis for daily service requirements and this policy led to many small buildings at the pit bank, housing lamprooms, stables and maintenance tradesmen. Steam-powered air compressor units became a feature of most new collieries, the air used to power underground machinery. To give economy of handling coal and supplies on the surface, many small tramways connected the pit bank with stockyards, boilers and distribution points on the arterial tramways.

The exclusive use of hand coal getting, and the many orders concerning the cleaning of the coal at the face, meant that very little preparation for market was needed. However, the more stringent consumer requirements as to grade of fuel and its size did demand that efforts be made to segregate stocks accordingly, and screens to graduate the size of coal came to be introduced at some of the pits. These tended to be the pits sending supplies out via the tramways; Coppice Field had screens fitted in 1863, the reason being that a full tram of a particular size could be despatched. Coal screens also had to be provided at the teeming or loading points on the canal at Worsley and Boothsbank. The primitive shaker screens used had a steam plant to drive them, and relied heavily upon the Walkden yard staff to maintain them.

A job that actively united the collieries and canals for a purpose other than carrying coal came as an annual event. Each year during July and August, when trade naturally slackened owing to reduced domestic demand, the opportunity was taken to clean out the canal bed. Gangs of up to 200 colliers, under the charge of pit underlookers, were set to dredging sludge from a drained section of the canal. The length from Sale to Leigh was done in sections, the whole process taking a few weeks.

The west entrance tunnel at Worsley. So much came from so little

Deeper Pits and Railways

The most noticeable change in the working of the Trust's collieries in the late 1860s and early 1870s came in the method of transporting the mined coal. With the Navigable Level system it had in the past been natural to use water transport when economic. Unfortunately, the bulk of the output now came from pits without adequate connections to the system. To maintain continuity of supply to the Bridgewater Canal, the two tramways built in the 1830s had extensions laid to the newer pits as they came into production.

On the west side of the coalfield, the Ellenbrook tramroad ran for one-and-a-quarter miles from Hilton Lane, crossed the Newearth Road at Mather Fold and reached the canal at Boothsbank. Subsequently, during the 1840s, a branch ran for half a mile from a junction near Mather Fold to City and Gatley pits in New Manchester. With the opening of Madams Wood pits in 1850, a further half mile extension joining the Gatley branch had to be laid and this section also served the Ellenbrook pits. The junction of these two branches is marked by a stone carved to record the death of a dog, run over by a coal tram. Such a volume of traffic used this tramway that four pass-bys were needed in the single track line south of Ellenbrook Church. To regulate traffic on the line, a signal to safeguard road users came to be installed at the level crossing over Newearth Road in 1862.

Serving the other flank of the Trust's lands, the Wardley tramroad originally connected Sanderson's pits at Roe Green with the canal at Worsley, a fairly straight line of three-quarters of a mile. During the late 1840s this tramroad had to be extended a further mile to serve Coppice Field and Hollins Field pits sunk near the turnpike road (A6) north-east of Wardley Hall. On completion of the Linnyshaw pit in 1860 the tramway had to be extended under the highway to reach it, making the total length two and a quarter miles. Owing to the steepness of the incline of the first quarter-mile section of this line from the canal, it had been worked as an inclined

plane with ropes and brake wheel. However, capacity increased to the point where a stationary engine had to be provided to operate the haulage.

The trams used on both these lines carried about 3 tons of coal and were solidly built for the purpose. The brake mechanism was well up to its task of controlling the freewheeling loaded descent of the line, and operated by a brakesman on each tram. On reaching the canal loading point they could discharge from either end or bottom doors.

Useful and hard worked though

they were, these five miles of horse tramways only fed the Trustees' canal. Further, the use of horses restricted capacity when the Trust's wish was to increase output. As major canal proprietors, the Trust were only too well aware of the competitive advantage railways gave over canals in transporting coal and despite their previous opposition to railways in all forms, realisation came that change was inevitable. The London & North Western Railway, in which Lord Stafford had much influence, was encouraged to build a railway line through Eccles and Worsley to Wigan. This opened in 1864 and was welcomed as a means of distributing Worsley coal.

The Trust then undertook the

The railway wagon tippler for loading canal boats at Worsley basin

modernisation of their internal transport arrangements. Broadly, they planned to link the main new collieries by a standard gauge steam traction railway, which was to take the form of two arms meeting in the north and connecting with the L.N.W.R. and the canal. These railways generally followed the route of the old tramways, but were not superimposed on them.

The first contract was let in 1865 to John Clarridge of Swinton and involved a line from Buckley Lane to Linnyshaw colliery, with a spur to Ashton's Field. One of the main features of the line was an embankment across the Blackleach reservoir, which had by then been extended to cover an area of 25 acres. Relatively few earthworks were needed to cross Linnyshaw Moss. A further contract extended the line south, with a cutting under the A6 road, to the Bridgewater colliery, where sidings and loading stages were built. The last section of this arm had not been completed to Sanderson's sidings on the L.N.W.R., nor to the canal, when locomotives of the 0-6-0 type were delivered in July and September 1870. These had to be horse hauled to their shed at Bridgewater colliery.

During the years 1870-71 work was begun on the other arm of the

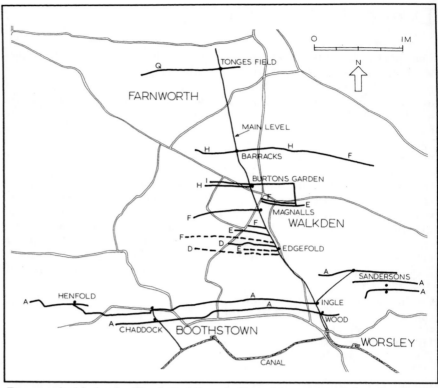

Deep navigable levels. The dotted lines indicate lower, second deep levels. (See seam sequence chart, page 2)

railway from Boothsbank on the canal northwards to Mosley Common colliery. A connection was made to the L.N.W.R. at Ellenbrook, and the line continued on an embankment to the Ellesmere colliery in Walkden. A gathering of officials inspected this section on its opening in October 1871. The final contract for the basic Trustees' line was tendered in July 1872 and was for the section to join Ellesmere and Ashton's Field pits. On the opening of the L.N.W.R. branch line from Roe Green to Little Hulton, connection was made with this near Ellesmere pits; similarly a connection was laid from the Linnyshaw line to the Lancashire & Yorkshire Railway's new Kearsley mineral line in the late 1870s.

The power base of the Trustees' holdings also altered radically in the early 1870s. Faced with increasing railway competition for traffic on their canals, which was highlighted by their own increased use of railways, capital could not be found to develop both the mines and the canals. The Trust therefore took the step of selling the canals and docks.

A consortium of railway directors formed the Bridgewater Navigation Company and purchased the canals and all the navigation interests of the Trust for £1,200,000. The negotiations to form the new company and obtain an Act of Parliament to change the terms of the Trust occupied the years 1872-74. The Trust did maintain a boatyard and a fleet of boats for coal haulage, based at Worsley, and made constant use of

This tramway engine house behind Sefton Drive, Worsley, contained the stationary engine for haulage on the steep incline to the canal at Worsley

the coal wharfs at Boothsbank and Worsley at their railway termini, but that was the extent of their interest.

After the sale of the canals, the Trustees were left with the estate and mineral rights at Worsley, the colliery undertakings and a sound financial base. The remaining assets were undoubtedly the most profitable of the concern. Just prior to the sale, in 1868-69, the Trust opened their new headquarters, a purpose-built office block in the centre of Walkden which housed all the administrative departments. The superintendent, general manager and the colliery agent were there, and those who served the collieries generally also had their base in the building - the surveyors and, perhaps the most important, a sales department. In later years the headquarters were connected by telegraph to the collieries, the Manchester sales office and the Trust's many other sales agents in the industrial North.

The works yard at Walkden, which had always served the collieries, gained in importance over the old canal depot at Worsley after the sale of the canals. As a central works depot for the engineering services required by the collieries, its composition reflected the

growing significance of this service. It possessed a large and well equipped machine shop, a smithy and a millwright's or fitter's shop.

These shops were responsible for the repair of the capital plant, which was being used in greater quantities in the last quarter of the century, and also housed the many experimental coal cutting devices the Trust tested or tried to develop. Quite a lot of the colliery surface structures were timber-built so a sawmill and joiner's shop continued in use, as did the masons' sheds and mortar mills. Transport equipment featured high in the overall cost of coal, particularly after the introduction of the railway, so it is perhaps natural that a wagon machine shop, a wheelwright's shop and a sleeper creosoting plant found a home at Walkden yard.

The last quarter of the nineteenth century saw the number of the Trust's active shafts contract, but there was a tremendous increase in output and in the number of employees. In the early 1850s about 25 pits, some small, others newer sinkings with multiple shafts, and a few active branch levels employed about 1,500 people, producing 278,000 tons. By the close of the century, just 8 fully

productive pits had a labour force of over 4,000, excluding transport and ancillary workers, with a peak production in 1890 of 1,400,000 tons.

The transition occupied virtually all the 1870s. As the new deep pits took time to open up their productive capacity fully and provide adequate work places, the medium pits struggled on, despite their state of near exhaustion in the late 1860s. In mid-decade the rush of closures of the old pits started, with a corresponding increase of labour force at the new. Tonge's Field ceased winding in 1875, as did the interdependent pits of Madams Wood and Magnall's, although the latter pit retained its pumping function. The remaining deep level workings at the Barracks pit were abandoned by 1876, with the colliers being transferred to the Ellesmere colliery. Next came the closure of two more pits connected by a deep navigable level, Edgefold and the Gatley pits, but again Edgefold maintained its pumping capacity to protect the workings of Mosley Common. Each of the Burgess Land pits also closed in 1877. The closures left about ten active collieries, either served by the Trustees' railway or with fairly adequate road links such as in the Watergate area. Productive capacity outstripped that of the

Ashton's Field Colliery. The Trustees developed deep workings alongside the Navigable Level

previous decade, but did not match demand.

Additional capacity was provided at Mosley Common colliery with the sinking of No.4 and No.5 shafts in 1878-79. No.4 shaft was sunk to work the Trencherbone seam at 580 yards, and No.3 shaft was deepened to this seam also, and converted from a ventilation to a winding and upcast shaft. The No.5 shaft, 250 yards deep, was to be the main ventilating shaft after working connections were made from the existing No.1 and 2 pits. By the time these developments had been opened up to provide adequate work places, the transfer of colliers from the nearby Ellenbrook pits had started. As Ellenbrook was not directly served by the Trust's railway, the coal from there had been sent down the only remaining section of horse tramways to the railway at Mather Fold, where an interchange took place. On the final closure of Ellenbrook pits in 1886, the tram track was lifted and used in the Trust's brickyard near Mosley Common.

The distribution of the pits left the Middle Hulton district unworked at a deep level until, in 1878, work started on sinking a new pit in the

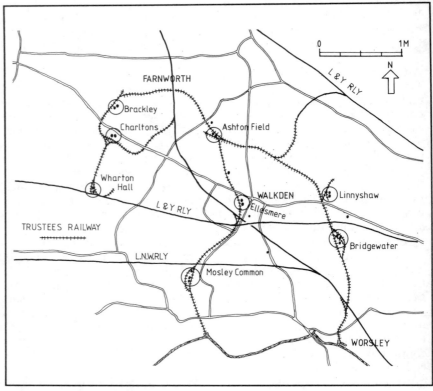

Collieries and transport 1890-1900

area. Brackley colliery comprised shafts sunk initially to the Plodder and Dean Moor seams and later deepened to the Arley seam 310 yards down. These had the (by then) usual high pressure steam engines and steel lattice headgear.

A further entry point was a sloping 'day eye', driven at 1 in 4 gradient down to the Plodder seam. Eventually, pumping of the extensive workings was facilitated by a connection to the branch navigable level in the Cannel seam.

Potential capacity increased in the 1880s with the re-purchase of the Wharton estate in Middle Hulton, including two collieries adjacent to the A6 formerly worked by the Charlton family. These were taken over and continued working the Cannel seam without any major alterations to the plant until the abandonment of the pits in 1898.

Also included in the Wharton Estate were Wharton Hall pits, extensively developed by the Trust from 1862. No.1 pit was sunk 305 yards to the Cannel seam and given a timber headframe, whilst No. 2 pit reached 550 yards deep to the Arley seam. This shaft had a steel headframe, and both shafts were 14 feet in diameter. No.3 pit, only 11 feet in diameter, was 435 yards deep, and had a timber headframe. The two main shafts had new engines and boiler ranges fitted, which together with an improved fan and coal screens resulted in a very efficient colliery.

Ellesmere pit, Walkden town centre, originally had Navigable Level and rail transport for its coal

These pits in the Middle Hulton district had their own railway system, connecting the three pits with the L.&Y.R. and the L.N.W.R. Eventually a link was made between Brackley and Ashton's Field pits, fully interconnecting each of the Trustees' pits.

The extensive nature of this private railway proved of commercial benefit in many ways. Its multiple connections with the two railway companies allowed the most advantageous route and tariff to be selected in despatching coal to consumers.

By 1890 the Trust's collieries had been consolidated into a modern productive unit by the standards of the time. Very few of the previous methods of working remained, with the exception of the Navigable Level. With the increased reliance on rail transport and the fact that less than a quarter of the total output came from pits connected with it, the use of the Level for coal transport finally ceased in 1887 - as a transport route it had been an anachronism from about 1870. It did, however, retain its utility as a drainage unit, receiving the discharge from the pumps of Brackley, Ashton's Field and Ellesmere. Pumping capacity to protect the current workings was maintained at Magnall's and Edgefold, which, together with the natural flow of water from the

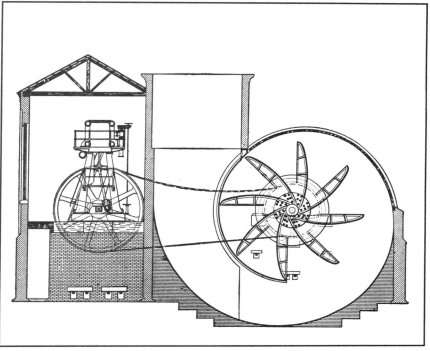

The ventilation fan manufactured by Walker Brothers of Wigan, as used in the larger Bridgewater pits

abandoned branch levels, gave a great saving in pump capacity at the deep pits.

As the collieries underwent the process of transition to a few pits, but with a much increased workforce, so the means of supervision also changed. In the years of railway building, the

roving commission of Thomas Wallwork as overall manager giving advice to underlookers and reporting to the agent had become impractical. The pits were split into geographical groupings with a manager, usually the former senior underlooker, appointed at each pit. These men reported to the district managers, who in turn were responsible to the agent at Walkden. The districts eventually resolved themselves as follows:

No.1: Mosley Common and Edgefold pumping station

No.2: Linnyshaw, Ellesmere and Ashton's Field

No.3: Brackley, Charlton's and Wharton Hall

No.4: Bridgewater

One of the factors allowing the remarkable increase in output from the collieries in the last decade of the century was increased mechanisation. It is true that the labour force had grown in proportion to output, but the increase was largely in the number of colliers, not haulage hands. Numerous experiments at mechanical coal cutting had made little headway during the 1880s, although various mining equipment companies produced relatively efficient units of both the toothed disc and the bar type for undercutting the coal. By the end

Trustees' Walkden yard fire brigade also covered the collieries and was on ? the neighbourhood

of the century several of both types were in use at each colliery, but contributed only a small proportion of the pits' output.

However, increased use of powered underground haulage is noticeable throughout these years. Both the down-shaft, rope-gearing type and underground, compressed-air, motor types of machine were used. These features, and the use of multi-deck cages raising steel tubs, fully justified the heavy expenditure on them. The 1880s also saw the transition from furnaces to fans for ventilating the extensive workings and by the turn of the century each working pit had its centrifugal fan driven by a steam engine. As a comparison, the old Guibal unit at Buckley Lane, venting Ashton's Field, was 30ft diameter x 10ft wide, whilst the more efficient Scherle fan at Brackley was only 10ft diameter x 3ft 6in wide.

Whilst the colliers were still required to produce as clean a coal as possible, more reliance was placed on surface treatment to suit an ever more discerning market. Each of the pits came to be provided with powered shaker screens to size the product, coupled with picking belts. At these belts, youths and disabled

Jesse Wallwork, mining agent to the Bridgewater Trust and Earl of Ellesmere; Managing Director of Bridgewater Collieries

colliers removed any shale as the coal passed, and this development naturally led to the need to dump the shale. Heaps formed alongside several of the pits and in later years the bulk of this spoil was taken by rail to Cutacre tip near Wharton Hall, to make one of the largest spoil heaps in Lancashire.

Coke production had featured in the revenue-earning account since the early years of the Duke's expansion. Its manufacture had been spread between Dixon Green, Walkden and Worsley, and whilst these ovens continued in use until the mid-1880s, the plant was of obsolete design. With the opening of Brackley colliery and its connection to the railway, a new by-product plant and coke works was built there. Based on the latest type of plant, this had its own coal washers capable of dealing with 30 tons per hour. The ovens were in two banks of 25, each oven 30 feet by 16 inches, of the Semet type. Coke grading screens were also installed. Eventually, town's gas was also produced to supply Little Hulton, and this township's council was the first to obtain Parliamentary authority to use gas made at cokeworks.

Shunters in Walkden sidings about 1900

Winding up

The Trust, administering the Worsley estates and collieries set up under the terms of the Duke of Bridgewater's will, had reached the end of its allotted time by 1903. From October that year all assets were turned over to the Earl of Ellesmere as sole owner, not merely the beneficiary. In terms of administration, Captain Hart-Davis, as the Earl's agent, undertook the duties of the Trust's superintendent. There were few other changes in personnel and the collieries continued under the direction of Mr J Wallwork.

As reported in a newspaper article in 1911, the collieries could truly be said to be at the height of their prosperity with a bright future. Despite the long history of working, the article noted that they had the largest unworked reserves in Lancashire, as well as being one of the largest colliery concerns in the country. The productive collieries were Mosley Common, Brackley, Wharton Hall, Bridgewater, Ellesmere, Linnyshaw and Ashton's Field. These comprised 13 shafts drawing coal, with 6 ventilation shafts. There were also the pumping stations of Magnall's and Edgefold, together with the remaining Main Navigable Level

Edgefold Pit being demolished in 1968

as a drainage unit. The newspaper article further noted that the most up-to-date equipment and processes were used at these collieries.

Owing to economic circumstances, the Ellesmere family severed connections with the Worsley concerns in 1923. Ownership of the collieries and estates came to be in the control of a joint stock company and the main holding company, Bridgewater Estates Ltd, formed many subsidiaries to run the various interdependent activities.

The pits were grouped as Bridgewater Collieries Ltd, with Mr Jesse Wallwork as managing director, and the Trustees' offices continued to be used as headquarters. Most of the coal sales organisation was absorbed as Bridgewater Wharves Ltd.

Unfortunately the bright future prophesied in 1911 did not materialise. National economic depression hit the coal industry particularly hard, causing the closure of many pits that had only marginal profitability. Ellesmere pit ceased production in 1923, but

Ashton's Field Pit in the 1960s, with conveyors installed for the coal blending plant on the site

retaining its pumping function to protect other workings. Ashton's Field and Linnyshaw also closed in the 1920s, the former being maintained for access to the old navigable levels.

During 1929 an amalgamation of many local firms took place and Bridgewater Collieries Ltd was one of the ten private companies that formed Manchester Collieries Ltd, in an attempt to strengthen their trading position. Initially the constituent companies retained a great deal of autonomy, but by 1935 central control had been fully established. This centralisation of production tied in with the new central sales organisation set up with Government approval in 1930. Lancashire Associated Collieries, based at Worsley Old Hall, acted in the interests of Lancashire coal owners against coal owners from other districts and retained this function until nationalisation.

During the period of Manchester Collieries many arrangements were made to work in conjunction with neighbouring pits, often ones which had formerly been owned separately. Mosley Common workings were connected to Astley Green pit and Bridgewater (Sandhole) was connected with

Mosley Common No.3 Pit skip winding unit, built after nationalisation

and partly ventilated Newtown and Pendlebury. These last two collieries were also linked to the private railway network. Wharton Hall pits had by now been converted to a pumping station to protect the Brackley workings.

Underground, one of the main changes was the more widespread

use of mechanical cutters to undercut the coal. Electric lighting had also come into general use at pit bottoms, as had electric signalling on the rope haulages, some of which were electric-driven.

On nationalisation on 1st January 1947, only three of the 'Bridgewater' pits remained as coal

Mosley Common Colliery about 1960, showing friction winder and washery

producers: Brackley, Mosley Common and Bridgewater, by this time officially known as Sandhole. Four of the old pits remained in use as pumping stations and the Main Navigable Level and several branches were also maintained for drainage, some 11,500,000 gallons per year being discharged from them.

Throughout their remaining life under the N.C.B., Brackley and Bridgewater pits continued without major alterations to shafts or surface plant. Up-to-date methods and machinery were absorbed underground and suitable welfare facilities provided.

The real changes occurred at Mosley Common. During the late 1950s and early 1960s the colliery was virtually reconstructed. Shafts were deepened to 1,000 yards and widened to 22ft diameter. Electric

Mosley Common No.2 Pit winding engine, typical of the later generation of equipment

winding engines and headgear were installed. Here all the latest technology came to be used, in mechanised faces, skip winding and extensive coal preparation plant. Mosley Common became the show pit of Lancashire.

Unfortunately market forces - the use of oil fuels and geological problems - eventually defeated the N.C.B. at the Worsley coalfield. Bridgewater (Sandhole) closed in September 1962, followed by Brackley in May 1964, and this closure also meant the final abandonment of Wharton Hall pits in 1964. Pumping also ceased at Ashton's Field in 1966, the water being allowed to fill the old workings and drain naturally into the Level, so that the Level north of Ashton's Field was then abandoned.

Despite all the investment, Mosley Common closed in February 1968, the last working 'Bridgewater' pit in the area. The remaining pumping stations on the old Level, Ellesmere and Edgefold, were abandoned and filled. Complete abandonment of the Level was planned, with the entrance at the delph closed with concrete sills in order to raise the water level to give a gas seal and prevent entry. However, the trapped gas escaped through capped shafts, causing problems, so the sills had to be removed and through ventilation restored.

It is perhaps fitting that the Navigable Level, the first of the great works at the coalfield, should have been the last to be fully abandoned.

Brackley Colliery after closure

Appendix 1

The Extent of the Navigable Levels

Seam intercepts listed south to north. Distances in yards.

Level or seam branch	Branch to West	North/South Level	Branch to East	Total Distance
Highest Cannel	2,040		700	2,740
UPPER LEVEL		3,350		
Black seam	1,160		370	
Doe seam	400		380	
Five Quarters seam	300		300	
Cannel seam	3,600		500	
Plodder seam	900		-	
Dean Moor seam	4,635		350	16,245
MAIN LEVEL		6,300		
Main Level West Entrance		500		
Four Foot seam	2,760		960	
Tunnel			460	
Three Quarter seam	440		-	
1st Binn seam	660		-	
1st Croumbouke seam	460		-	
1st Brassey seam	400		-	
1st Seven Feet seam	320		120	
2nd Binn seam	580		360	
2nd Croumbouke seam	-		780	
2nd Seven Feet seam	-		1,350	
1st Black seam	520		930	
1st Black cont. in White seam	520		660	
1st Black cont. in Five Quarters	-		280	
1st Doe seam	1,360		650	
1st Doe cont. in 3rd Seven Feet			480	
1st Five Quarters seam	220		1,060	
1st Five Quarters cont. in 4th Binn			990	
1st Five Quarters cont. in 4th Croum.			1,400	
1st Five Quarters cont. in 4th Brassey			600	
1st Five Quarters cont. in Seven Feet			500	
2nd Black seam	1,220		560	
2nd Doe seam	1,600		620	
2nd Doe cont. in Black & White			220	
2nd Five Quarters seam	500		520	
Cannel seam	3,860		350	
Plodder seam	190		-	
Dean Moor seam	4,400		1,320	41,980
DEEP LEVELS				
Wood Pit - 4 Foot seam	2,134		330	
Ingle Pit - 4 Foot seam	2,772		-	
Roe Green - 4 Foot seam			1,540	
Edgefold Pit 1st Deep		330		
Edgefold Pit Croumbouke seam	968		-	
Edgefold Pit Brassey seam	836		-	
Edgefold Pit Seven Feet seam	396		-	
Edgefold Pit 2nd Deep		264		
Edgefold Pit Croumbouke seam	1,694		-	
Edgefold Pit Brassey seam	660		-	
Edgefold Pit Seven Feet seam	1,760		-	
Magnall's Pit Seven Feet seam	1,254		-	
Burton's Garden Pit		70		
Burton's White seam	880		-	
Burton's Black seam	770		880	
Burton's Tunnel		396		
Burton's Brassey seam			770	
Burton's Seven Feet seam			550	
Barracks Pit White seam	814		1,100	
Barracks Pit Seven Feet seam			1,606	
Tonge's Field Pit Dean Moor	1,562		396	24,732
CHADDOCK LEVEL		968		
Chaddock Pit Four Foot seam	814		1,078	
Queen Anne Four Foot seam	902		506	
Henfold Pit Four Foot seam	1,914			6,182

OVERALL TOTALS

High Cannel Level	2,740	yards =	1m	4f	5ch
Upper Level and Branches	16,245	yards =	9m	1f	8ch
Main Level and Branches	41,980	yards =	23m	6f	8ch
Deep Levels	24,732	yards =	14m	0f	4ch
Chaddock Level and Branches	6,182	yards =	3m	4f	1ch
			52m	**1f**	**6ch**

Output

Appendix 2
Shaft Register

This list indicates when the shafts named were first mentioned in the surviving documents of the Duke's and Trust's records. It does not confirm the date of sinking, unless this is specifically given in the text. The intention is to show the amazing number of shafts sunk and the start of their period of prominence. Many ventilation shafts and ladder pits are not listed, as minor works were not always recorded in a form that aids identification. The locations are approximate.

NL = Navigable Level access, W = winding, P = pumping, V = ventilation

1760 - 1770
Little Ladyhill	NL	Worsley
Great Ladyhill	NL	Worsley
Cannel Engine	W	Dixon Green
Cookes Meadow	W	Ellenbrook
Cookes Meadow	P	Ellenbrook
Cookes Meadow	V	Ellenbrook
Clays	NL	Ellenbrook
Prices		Walkden
Speakmans		Walkden
Edgefold		Walkden
Lloydes		Walkden
Heys Field		Walkden
Grundy Common		Ellenbrook

1770 - 1780
Kempnough	Worsley
Turnpike Lime (2 shafts)	Walkden
Barlow Fold	Walkden
Scowcrofts	Walkden
Crippins Croft	Walkden
Stones Croft	Dixon Green
Watsons Croft	Dixon Green
Lawtons Croft	Dixon Green
Cromptons Croft	Dixon Green
Holmes Croft	Dixon Green

1780 - 1790
Ingles	Worsley
Pin Fold	Walkden
Parr Fold	Walkden
Tub Engine	Walkden
Machine	Dixon Green
Tonges Field	Dixon Green
Tonges Meadow (2 shafts)	Dixon Green
Green Ashes Croft	Dixon Green

1790 - 1800
Lumber Lane	V	Roe Green
Grundys Field		Walkden
Stone	NL	Walkden
Windmill	NL	Walkden
Charltons	NL	Walkden
Inclined Plane Pit	NL	Walkden
Coke Oven	NL	Walkden
Buckley Lane	NL	Farnworth
Doe Pit	NL	Farnworth

1800 - 1810
Urmstons Meadow	Walkden
Moss - Hill Top	Walkden
Parkinsons	Walkden
Sawney	Walkden
Turnpike	Wardley
Eckersleys Croft	Deane
Culbert Field	Deane
Smethursts	Deane
Scott Meadow	Deane
Lomas's Lane	Deane

1810 - 1820
Chaddock (2 shafts)	Chaddock
Cowshill Meadow	Chaddock
Henfold	Chaddock
Common	Ellenbrook
Swiney Lane	Ellenbrook
Millhough	Ellenbrook
Atkins Croft	Walkden
Wood (2 shafts)	Worsley
Gate	Farnworth

1820 - 1830
Cinder Field	Wardley
Dornings	Wardley
Worsleys	Wardley
Hollins	Wardley
Moss	Linnyshaw
Burtons Garden	Walkden
Frays Field	Hulton

1830 - 1840
Sandersons	W	Roe Green
Sandersons	P	Walkden
Barracks		Walkden
Magnalls		Walkden
Lansdales Field		Wardley
Lords Moss		Dixon Green
Howarths Field		Deane
Watergate		Deane
Sapling Field		Deane
Fletchers Field		Deane
Burgess Land (3 shafts)		Little Hulton
Hilton Lane (2 shafts)		Little Hulton
Tynesbank		Little Hulton
Foumes Bank		Ellenbrook
Mathers Field		Ellenbrook

1840 - 1850
Tonges Field	Dixon Green
Gatley (2 shafts)	Ellenbrook
Coppice Field (3 shafts)	Wardley
Madams Wood (2 shafts)	Little Hulton

Delph	Deane
Coke Oven	Walkden

1850 - 1860
Buckley Lane	Farnworth
Ashtons Field (2 shafts)	Walkden
Linnyshaw (2 shafts)	Wardley

1860 - 1870
Mosley Common	W	Ellenbrook
Mosley Common	P	Ellenbrook
Mosley Common	V	Ellenbrook
Ellesmere	W	Walkden
Ellesmere	W/P	Walkden
Ellenbrook (2 shafts)	W	Ellenbrook
Bridgewater	W	Wardley
Bridgewater	W/P	Wardley

1870 - 1880
Mosley Common	W	Ellenbrook
Mosley Common	V	Ellenbrook
Brackley (2 shafts)	W	Little Hulton
Brackley Day Eye		Little Hulton
Bridgewater	W	Wardley

1880 - 1890
Charltons (2 shafts)	Little Hulton
Wharton Hall (2 shafts)	Little Hulton

Appendix 3
Colliery Equipment about 1830

M Boats	82
T Boats	75
Boats in Lower Levels	45
Steam Engines	4
Tub Engines	9
Horse Gins	10

Appendix 4
Colliery Equipment and Employees about 1840

Depth in yards. EF = Engine Function, hp/ty = horsepower or type.
T = Tunnellers, C = Colliers, B = Boys, G = Girls, Bo = Boatmen

Colliery	Depth	EF	hp/ty	T	C	B	G	Bo
Chaddock Engine Pit	121	Pump	70					
Chaddock Coal Pit	120	Winding	14		40	40	30	14
Higher Chaddock Coal Pit	80	Winding	12		14	15	5	5
Sandersons Pit	144	Wind+Pump	26	15	21	23	7	2
Edgefold Engine Pit	129	Pump	26					
Edgefold Coal Pit	128	Winding	Water balance	16	30	29	13	3
Burtons Garden	114	Winding	Water balance		25	26	14	4
Barracks Pit	144	Wind+Pump	27	5	41	38	29	4
Lords Moss	132	Wind+Pump	16	14				
Howarths Field	51		Gin wheel		16	16		
Watergate	84	Winding	6		26	2		
Cannel Mine				10	70	24		11
Deane Moor Mine				22	92	155		10
Sapling Field	124	Winding	8		9	4		
Culbert Field	62	Winding	8		13	7	1	
Eckersleys Field	80	Pumping	12		10	10		
Hilton Lane	74	Wind+Pump	8		8	8	4	
Burgess Land No.1	83	Winding	6		10	8	7	
Burgess Land No.2	99				14	13	8	
Burgess Land No.3	36	Winding	Gin wheel		11	9	8	
Mathers Field	32	Winding	14	6				
Magnalls		Pumping	50	9				
Magnalls		Winding	16	9				
Linnyshaw Pit	154	Wind+Pump	16	2	16	24	4	
Cinder Field	110	Wind+Pump	14		21	14	8	
Hollins Field	106				19	19	5	
Dornings Field	102	Wind+Pump	20					
Worsleys Field	96	Winding	6		11	10	1	
Lansdales Field		Wind+Pump	28	10				

Appendix 5

Colliery Equipment about 1900

Ashton's Field

No.1 Pit: 10ft diameter x 336 yards deep, 4 wood guides, wood trestle headgear, engine horizontal duplex 30in x 60in stroke, 640hp.
No.2 Pit: 12ft diameter x 567 yards deep, 4 wood guides, wood trestle headgear, engine vertical pair 30in x 60in stroke.
Seams worked: Dean Moor, Plodder, Arley. Coal tubs: 1,290. Lamps: 400. Coal cutting machines: No.1 Pit 7, No.2 Pit 4. Underground haulage: Endless rope and main rope or direct haulage electrically driven. Subsidiary compressed air engines. Pumping: 10 million gallons per year to Navigable Level. Compressed air and electric pumps. Surface plant: 5 Lancashire boilers, air compressor engine horizontal compound, 23in and 41in diameter x 42in stroke. 3 jigging or vibrating screens, 3 picking belts 46ft long, 3ft wide, with 22hp electric drive.

Buckley Lane Ventilating Station

Shaft: 10ft diameter x 285 yards deep. Surface Plant: 2 Lancashire boilers. Fan: Guibal type 30ft diameter x 10ft wide, engine: horizontal duplicate 24in and 24in x 24in stroke.

Brackley

No.1 Pit: 14ft6in diameter x 310 yards deep. 6 guide rods, steel lattice headgear, engine horizontal pair 26in x 60in stroke.

No.2 Pit: 18ft6in diameter x 310 yards deep. 6 steel guides, wood trestle headgear, engine horizontal pair 20in x 42in stroke.
Day Eye: 10ft wide x 8ft high, 400 yds long, dip 1 in 4.
Seams worked: Cannel, Dean Moor, Three-Quarters, Arley. Coal tubs: 930 wood, 830 steel. Lamps: 600. Coal cutting machines: 6 disc, 13 bar. Underground haulage: Endless rope and main rope or direct haulage, electrically driven with subsidiary compressed air engines. Pumping: 30 million gallons per year to Navigable Level and surface use at coke works. Compressed air and electric pumps. Surface plant: 7 Lancashire boilers. Air compressor engine, two-stage cross compound 27in and 49in x 54in stroke. 3 jigging or vibrating screens. 3 picking belts, 78ft long, 3ft6in wide, multiple electric drives. Fan: Scherle type 10ft dia x 3ft 6in wide. Engine: pair horizontal 18in x 24in stroke.

Bridgewater (Sandhole)

No.1 Pit: 12ft diameter x 573 yards deep, 4 guide rods, steel lattice headgear, engine duplicate 30in x 60in stroke.
No.2 Pit: 12ft diameter x 590 yards deep, 8 guide rods, timber frame headgear, engine capstan type pair 11in x 31in stroke.
No.3 Pit: 14ft6in diameter x 329 yards deep, 4 guide rods, steel lattice headgear, engine pair horizontal 36in x 72in stroke.
Seams worked: Croumbouke, Seven Feet, Black, Hell Hole, Doe, Cannel. Coal tubs: 2,650 + 37 riding trams. Lamps: 850 safety + electric at pit bottom, etc. Coal cutting machines: 2. Underground haulage: Endless rope and main rope or direct haulage, electrically driven.

Brackley Colliery after closure

Pumping: 75 million gallons per year to surface. Turbine high lift pump. 500 g.p.m. at 960ft hd. 240hp electric motor. Surface plant: 6 Lancashire boilers. Air compressor engine duplex 26in x 48in stroke (serve No.1 & No.2 pits). 7 Lancashire boilers. Air compressor engine duplex 24in x 48in stroke (serve No.3 pit). 2 sets screens: 2 vibrating type. Three 60ft picking belts. Steam engine driven pair 15in x 24in stroke. Also washery with slack washing troughs and revolving screens. Fan: Walker type 24ft diameter x 8ft wide. Engine horizontal compound 21in and 36in x 42in stroke.

Hollins Field Ventilation Station
Shaft: 12ft diameter x 465 yards deep. Timber headframe. Plant: Cornish boiler, single cylinder engine. Flat rope winding.

Ellesmere
No.1 Pit: 12ft diameter x 276 yards deep. 2 wood guides, timber trestle headgear. Engine 1 pair vertical 30in x 54in stroke.
No.2 Pit: 12ft diameter x 415 yards deep. 4 steel rope guides, steel lattice headgear. Engine 1 pair vertical 30in x 54in stroke.
Seams worked: Five Quarters, Seven Feet, Black, Doe, Trencherbone, Cannel. Coal tubs: 870. Safety lamps: 300. Underground haulage: Surface engine pair 20in x 48in. Endless rope down shaft to clutch in seam. Subsidiary compressed air engines and electric drives. Pumping: 110 million gallons per year to Navigable Level. Surface plant: 4 Lancashire boilers. Air compressor unit. Four vibrating screens and picking belts 78ft long. Driving engine: pair 10in x 16in stroke.

Ellesmere Ventilating Station
Shaft: 12ft diameter x 255 yards deep. Fan: Sirocco type 13ft diameter x 4ft6in wide. Drive by 60hp electric motor.

Edgefold Pumping Station
No.1 Pit: Winding: 8ft diameter x 178 yards deep. 1 deck cage, timber headgear, engine single 18in x 36in stroke.
No.2 Pit: Pumping: 6ft and 8ft diameter x 181 yards deep. Timber sheerlegs, capstan engine 9in x 18in. Pumping: 30 million gallons per year to Navigable Level. Engine: Vertical Bull type 42in x 84in stroke, cast iron balance beam 14ft long. Pump lift of 11in diameter x 6ft stroke to cistern in shaft and Navigable Level. Plant: 2 Lancashire boilers.

Linnyshaw (Berryfield)
No.1 Pit: 10ft diameter x 300 yards deep, 2 wire guides, timber frame headgear, engine single cylinder 48in x 60in stroke.
No.2 Pit: 11ft diameter x 328 yards deep, timber frame headgear. Seams worked: Croumbouke, Brassey, Seven Feet. Coal Tubs: 1,500. Lamps: 260 safety and electric light at pit bottom. Underground haulage: Endless rope and main rope, direct haulage and subsidiary compressed air engines. Pumping: 23 million gallons per year to surface. Surface plant: Four Lancashire boilers. Air compressor engine pair 17in x 36in stroke. Three vibrating screens, 3 picking belts 25ft long x 3ft wide. Engine double horizontal 15in x 20in stroke. Fan: 15ft diameter x 5ft wide. Engine horizontal duplicate 21in x 36in stroke.

Wharton Hall
No.1 Pit: 14ft diameter x 305 yards deep, 4 wood guides, timber headgear, engine pair horizontal 26in x 60in stroke.
No.2 Pit: 14ft diameter x 555 yards deep, 6 steel guides, steel lattice headgear, engine pair horizontal 30in x 60in stroke.
No.3 Pit: 11ft diameter x 435 yards deep, wood guides, timber headgear, engine single vertical 10in x 18in stroke.
Seams worked: Seven Feet, Black, Cannel, Dean Moor, Arley. Coal tubs: 700. Lamps: safety 480, electric light at pit bottom. Coal cutting machines: 10.
Underground haulage: Endless rope and main rope, or direct haulage. Also subsidiary compressed air engines.
Pumping: 40 million gallons per year to surface. Surface plant: Five Lancashire boilers. Air compressor engines 2-stage compound 19in and 39in stroke, vibrating screens and picking belts 68ft long. Engine duplex 10in x 16in stroke. Fan: Scherle type 12ft6in diameter x 4in wide. Engine: single horizontal 20in x 36in duplicate engines.

Mosley Common
No.1 Pit: 12ft diameter x 343 yards deep, 4 wood guides, iron lattice headgear, engine pair vertical 32in x 48in stroke.
No.2 Pit: 12ft diameter x 529 yards deep, 8 wood guides, steel girder headgear, engine pair horizontal 36in x 66in stroke.
No.3 Pit: 12ft diameter x 551 yards deep, 4 rope guides, steel girder headgear, engine pair horizontal 30in x 60in stroke.
No.4 Pit: 18ft6in x 613 yards deep, 8 wire guides, steel lattice headgear, engine pair horizontal 40in x 72in stroke.
No.5 Pit: 12ft diameter x 253 yards deep, steel trestle headgear, capstan engine 12in x 20in stroke.
Seams worked: Croumbouke, Seven Feet, Doe, Trencherbone. Coal tubs: 3,700. Coal cutting machines: 5 disc and 4 bar types. Lamps: Electric at pit bottom, etc. 200 safety type. No.1 & No.2 Pits: 1,100, No.4 Pit: 600. Underground haulage: No.1 Pit: Endless rope and direct haulage, compressed air engines. No.2 Pit: Endless rope from engine on surface to Doe seam clutch. Subsidiary compressed air engines. No.4 Pit: Endless rope and main rope, compressed air engines.
Pumping: 70 million gallons per year to surface. Cornish pumping engine at No.1 Pit. Cylinder 51in x 72in stroke, which worked at four-and-a-half strokes per minute, pump ram 14in diameter. Surface plant: Lancashire boilers: 9 to Nos.1 & 2 Pits, 7 to No.4 Pit and 3 to Nos.3 and 5 pits. Air compressor engines: pair 26in x 48in stroke Nos.1 & 2 Pits: pair 26in x 48in stroke No.4 Pit. Screens: Nos.1 & 2 Pits: 4 vibrating screens, 4 picking belts 110ft long, 2 at 90ft long, engine pair 12in x 18in. No.4 Pit: 3 vibrating screens, 3 picking belts 100ft long, 1 at 170ft long, engine pair 10in x 18in and 1 at 7in x 12in. Fans: At No.4 Pit, Walker type 24ft diameter x 8ft wide, engine twin compound 22in and 38in x 48in stroke. At No.5 Pit, fan 15ft diameter x 5ft wide, engine twin compound 14in and 24in x 48in stroke.

Appendix 6
Coal Production 1760-1900

Owing to poor continuity in the surviving records, large gaps are apparent in this table. Many of the figures are based not on yearly output, but on records of coal sales via the canal, and allowance should be made for this.

Output in tons

Year	Output	Year	Output
1760		1830	165,634
1761		1831	178,161
1762		1832	174,260
1763		1833	220,369
1764	12,129	1834	229,421
1765	17,417	1835	271,840
1766	14,978	1836	283,631
1767	24,150	1837	269,825
1768	25,870	1838	259,714
1769	25,249	1839	274,459
1770	31,912	1840	262,724
1771	32,813	1841	254,117
1772	39,709	1842	
1773	36,981	1843	
1774	37,400	1844	282,678
1775	37,120	1845	279,212
1776	41,958	1846	307,649
1777	44,698	1847	270,084
1778	50,429	1848	254,030
1779	44,217	1849	281,822
1780	46,234	1850	278,713
1781	46,782	1851	
1782	52,204	1852	274,380
1783	48,491	1853	
1784	55,693	1854	
1785	50,986	1855	279,140
1786	51,362	1856	
1787	54,403	1857	
1788	60,184	1858	
1789	62,813	1859	
1790	69,660	1860	371,408
1791	93,807	1861	
1792	100,068	1862	
1793	111,646	1863	
1794	94,322	1864	
1795	110,224	1865	
1796	110,809	1866	
1797	119,056	1867	
1798	116,835	1868	
1799	127,449	1869	
1800	138,695	1870	
1801	144,044	1871	
1802	140,695	1872	
1803	134,035	1873	
1804	133,811	1874	
1805	127,192	1875	
1806	114,566	1876	
1807	109,071	1877	
1808	99,854	1878	
1809	99,034	1879	
1810	110,690	1880	
1811		1881	
1812		1882	
1813		1883	
1814		1884	
1815		1885	
1816		1886	1,303,625
1817		1887	1,345,192
1818		1888	1,404,474
1819		1889	1,403,244
1820		1890	1,410,379
1821		1891	1,422,999
1822		1892	1,389,322
1823		1893	922,597
1824		1894	1,229,408
1825		1895	1,088,516
1826		1896	994,377
1827		1897	991,670
1828		1898	
1829	153,630	1899	

Reference Sources
Primary sources

The surviving records of the Duke's estate, the Bridgewater Trust and subsequent companies, comprising account books, leases, royalty payments, salary and wage records. These, together with officials' reports, maps and mine plans form the basis of this study.

General account	1763-90	Lancs RO
General account	1790-1810	Lancs RO
Account of chief agent re collieries in Lancs	1759-1806	Northants RO
Day book	1769-70	Lancs RO
Cash account	1776	Lancs RO
Day book	1770-71	F Mullineux
Thos. Bury's Notebook	1778	Lancs Mining Museum
Cash book	1778-79	F Mullineux
Account book	1778-79	Lancs RO
Coal leases to 3rd Duke of Bridgewater to 1803		Lancs RO
Valuation of Capital	1803	Northants RO
Payments: Walkden Moor Colliery 1781-1817		Lancs Mining Museum
Coal Leases to Duke and Trustees 1790-1841		Northants RO
Accounts	1819-20	Lancs RO
General abstract of accounts	1829-37	Lancs RO
Annual departmental accounts	1844-50	Lancs RO
Colliery agents' correspondence	1807-57	Lancs RO
Coal leases by Bridgewater Trustees 1826-72		Lancs RO
List of steam and balance engines c1840		Lancs RO
Cash book: payments	1838-44	Lancs RO
Salaries journals	1824-42	Lancs RO
Prices paid for getting coal	1842-72	Lancs RO
Salaries journals	1843-86	Lancs RO
Daywage book	1848-60	Lancs RO
Daywage book	1863-69	Lancs RO
Daily Reports: Colliery Manager 1859-70		F Walsh
Correspondence re leases	1852-54	Lancs RO
Ellesmere Railway: Tenders and accounts 1865-72		Lancs RO
Colliery agents' notebooks	1873-78	Lancs RO
Correspondence: Social provisions	1837-71	Lancs RO
Salaries journals	1881-1900	Lancs RO
Colliery agent's letter book	1882-90	Lancs RO
Mine rents and royalties	1886-97	Lancs RO
Colliery valuation	1914	Lancs RO

The Duke's colliery plans: compiled 1760-1803

Key map of district with scale plans of each seam
N.C.B. Lowton

Plans of abandoned mines: Bridgewater Trust	N.C.B. Lowton
Shaft Register	N.C.B. Lowton
Worsley Estate Plan 1764	Lancs RO
Worsley Estate Plan 1840	Lancs RO
Worsley Estate Plan 1893	J Lane

Six-inch Ordnance Survey 1850

Geological Survey 1929

A collection of papers, mainly records of interviews with Mr J Wallwork, giving his recollections and other information concerning the Navigable Level. Collected during 1940-1970 by Mr J Lane.